GALVESTON'S *Red Light District*

A HISTORY OF THE LINE

Kimber Fountain

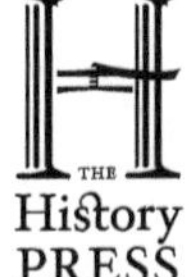

Published by The History Press
Charleston, SC
www.historypress.com

Front cover, background: author's personal collection: *foreground*: author's personal collection. *Back cover, top*: personal collection of Trey Click; *middle*: author's personal collection; *bottom*: courtesy of Rosenberg Library.

First published 2018

ISBN 9781540235688

Library of Congress Control Number: 2018940087

For my dad

CONTENTS

Contents

ACKNOWLEDGEMENTS

While writing *Galveston's Red Light District*, the words that Galveston's first elected female official, Ruth Kempner, said to a prominent madam often echoed through my mind, "But for the grace of God I would be in your house." In my case, that grace came in the form of my dad. Although he would never admit it, my dad is one of the biggest champions of equality that I know. The father of three daughters, he never once even hinted at the notion that my being female was a weakness. Because of this, my most valued possessions have always been my freedom and my independence, which, interestingly enough, were the same driving forces behind every woman who worked the Line. My dad never questioned that about me, he never told me I needed to "settle down," but what he did do was offer guidance that enabled me to productively channel this innate, rebellious desire to make my own rules and live the life I imagined.

John Hall, publisher of *Galveston Monthly* magazine, is truly one of the most talented people I know, and I consider working for him not only a pleasure but also an honor. I often tell readers of *Galveston Monthly* that we "bleed" into those pages, and sometimes it really does feel that way. He is the only person I know who loves Galveston more than I do, and his unceasing ability to conjure ideas never ceases to amaze me. His creativity, along with his constant support, have been two of the most influential factors in my career as a writer, and for that I am eternally grateful.

A special thank-you to Tena and Louie Jerger of the *Island Guide* for being the first to take a chance on an unpublished writer, and to The History Press, which did the same for an unpublished author.

Acknowledgements

To the wonderful staff at the Galveston and Texas History Center of the Rosenberg Library, especially Sean McConnell, for their generous assistance with my research.

To Scott Field and my other sources who preferred to stay anonymous, for lending me morsels of rare insight into an obscure part of Galveston history that were small but crucial to this story.

To Scotty Hanson, owner of Antique Warehouse at Twenty-Fifth Street and Postoffice. Three years ago, when I first wrote about the district for the magazine, Scotty was kind enough to regale me with a mountain of information about his building and the district, much of which I also used in this book.

Personally, I also owe an enormous amount of gratitude to my mom. She is not only the best mom I could have asked for, but she also bestowed upon me her love of grammar, reading and writing; she graciously gave of her English professor skills to edit my manuscript.

And to Eric, whose support of me is unending. I love you to the moon and back.

Lastly, I am fully convinced of the fact that we humans would be nothing without our dogs. Thus, I must acknowledge my sweet pea Elle; every day I strive to be the person that she thinks I am.

INTRODUCTION

I have always been one to root for the underdog, and if ever an underdog existed, it was a prostitute working the Line during the City of Galveston's torrid love affair with vice. She was the best kind of underdog, too—the kind that did not even know she was one. Most of these ladies were just doing what they had to do to survive or get ahead, and they felt lucky enough to be in a place that "let" them do it. To the select few who were not doing it out of necessity, it was likely more of a rebellious manifesto that proclaimed their own individual freedom than it was to be a symbol of midcentury activism. But whatever their reasons, these were women who valued their independence even more than they valued their dignity or place in society, and certainly more than an arbitrary moral code. These were women who saw themselves mired in a societal system that stacked the odds against them, giving them no other choice; they made that choice and made the best of it. These were women who I wanted to know.

Thus it became clear to me when assembling the structure of this book that I could not approach it like I have approached nearly every other piece of history I have written: chronologically. This format is certainly acceptable and useful, as recounting events, people and places in the order that they existed seems only natural. However, I knew that this work was an attempt to glean insight and garner understanding for a certain kind of woman who is often given no regard, as well as to ferret out the societal implications of her existence, and so I thought it wiser to fully establish the communal and economic environment in which she was immersed before presenting a case for her cultural vindication.

This structure also helped settle a minor internal conflict within myself that arises now and again in my work. I love history, and I love writing about it. Learning about how life used to be for the people who came before and tracing the steps of societal evolution are fascinating to me. However, I also hold a personal philosophy that the past is ultimately irrelevant, along the same lines of the gurus who teach "the past is in the past," "let go" and "your past doesn't define you." Thus, if I am to maintain that rehashing an individual's past is pointless, I must certainly find a very good reason for regurgitating the collective's.

Sometimes, my reason is simply to tell a story that has never been told or to recognize certain people whose contributions would otherwise be buried in the sands of time. Other times, I want to find the beauty and meaning in places where there was previously thought to be none, and I almost always seek to celebrate my subjects. With this particular subject, it was all of that and more.

I do not quite remember when I first learned of Galveston's red-light district, but I know that the moment I did was the moment I became enamored with the idea of it. I had been previously fascinated by stories of courtesans in Renaissance Italy, wonderfully portrayed in the 1997 movie *Dangerous Beauty* starring Catherine McCormack, and of course I, like every other person in the country, have seen *Pretty Woman* more times than I can count. When I found myself wanting to write a book about the topic, I could not help but wonder why it captivated me so much and why it did the same for most of the population. Why is prostitution an acceptable facet of mainstream pop culture, an appropriate scenario for a kitschy rom-com, yet the reality of it is feared and scorned to the point of inspiring movements against it? Is it illegal because it is immoral? Or is it illegal because the basis of it is completely misunderstood?

Meanwhile, I was catching my own little glimpse of the colossal stigma attached to prostitution. I often wondered what someone would think if they were to randomly discover my browser history or the list of books I had checked out from the library—fortunately, Rosenberg Library here in Galveston recently added automated checkout machines, and I was able to escape the curious stares that I was sure would be elicited from the librarian by the stack of books in my possession. I attributed the countless unreturned phone calls to the fact that I had been way too specific in my voicemails, and when I attempted to contact the few people who have researched and written about the Line, I found out that all of them have since passed away. On one occasion, a friend of mine gave me her uncle's phone number in the hopes he would have some information for me; I called him, but he passed away before he had a chance to call me back. I agreed to do anonymous interviews, because some people understandably did not want to publicly admit that they were privy to any firsthand information regarding prostitution in Galveston. At times, I felt like I was grasping at straws.

Suddenly, this became a rather daunting task: to lift a shroud of secrecy and shame that would reveal—what, exactly? Fortunately, the historic rabbit hole eventually produced more information than I could have hoped for, much of it firsthand and unspoiled by the distortion of memory or hearsay, and it led me precisely to the place that I had hoped to find. Interestingly, it was the same place that the story began for me, the root of that curiosity that I pondered: the humanity. The flesh and blood of that blurred line between black and white. The grit and grime of a life that was often primitive; the gaudy splendor of those not infrequent instances when it was anything but. Likewise, the mortal circumstances that prompted these women into the profession were just as divided as the results. Some were thrust into it by chance, others were running away from hopeless situations and still others were merely thrill seekers.

Underneath a tarnished legacy of scorn and ridicule were individuals whose only victims were themselves, and that was assuming that they even considered themselves victims, which the vast majority did not. Furthermore, an insatiably inelastic demand was in place long before the supply. These women knew that it was not the role of government, nor of law enforcement, nor of anyone else to protect them from themselves. Most important, the well-intentioned but false piety that disparaged these women and their choices was focused only on the symptom while completely ignoring the cancer. This was an era in which leaders were ludicrously diligent about propagating the arbitrary concept that a woman's only value is in her adeptness to domesticity, a time when even if she did manage to reach for more than motherhood, she was doing skilled work but being compensated less than an unskilled laborer. These are not radical interpretations of the past. They are facts. But they are not necessarily facts that must be used to place blame or underwrite judgment. Rather, to me, they are indications of how far we have come as a society, because in actuality, it was not the vigilante lawmen or the religious zealots who eradicated large-scale prostitution in Galveston—it was a shift in cultural norms that released women into the fray to realize their potential.

Additionally, this era of Galveston's existence also reveals the perils of prohibition and represents the basis of a tenet set forth by the Founding Fathers of the United States, who established this nation as a republic of states because they believed fundamentally in the state and local governments, as well as in the individual, to decide what was best for themselves and their communities. This country was instituted on the idea of ultimate emancipation; the *pursuit* of happiness, not happiness itself; freedom to succeed, but also freedom to fail; not to be a savior with unchecked permission to needlessly embellish public policy in order to control or feather the nest of every person born here.

Especially during a modern era when the country is experiencing egregious events of federal overreach that require licenses for basic rights and are continually locking up people for victimless crimes, coupled with third-wave feminism that has had a profoundly negative impact on the feminist cause (which was originally ignited, as previously indicated, by fundamental problems like suffrage and employment and educational opportunities), the tale of the Free State of Galveston and specifically its red-light district is an enlightening and entertaining vehicle to study these ideals.

Galveston never made prostitution legal, but it was certainly content to look the other way. Likewise, the women of the Line did not once protest or rally their cause or demand that city officials legalize their trade, yet for over sixty years, women regularly moved to Galveston to work in the district. They did not need a sanctioned validation of their lifestyle or a legislated endorsement of their career choice; they really only wanted one thing. Interestingly enough, it was the same thing that was then at the heart of Galveston's illicit economy and is today central to every feminist and anti-prohibition cause, something that when fully understood could revolutionize the way people see modern movements—they just wanted to be left alone.

PROLOGUE

The defining moments of Galveston's brief but splendid history are best illustrated by the evolution of the colorful subtitles that have been attached to the city's name at certain points along the course of its existence. Formally dubbed the namesake of the island upon which it dwells, the City of Galveston's historic journey has been fraught with as much peril as it has been laden with prosperity, but its nickname-inducing presence in the national spotlight has always highlighted the city's triumphs, and for good reason. The noteworthy accomplishments and frequent reclamations of its reputation were particularly deserved because they were, more often than not, born of equal or greater misfortune. Yet without calamity and disaster, without economic ruin and political strife, without being forced to question its identity time and time again, Galveston may never have become an "octopus" or a "playground." Without daring to question the status quo and challenge authority, it never would have been a Wall Street or a "free state."

Today, locals simply refer to it as paradise, although for many it may seem to fall short of such a lofty title. No doubt some islands have more temperate weather; whiter sands and bluer waters certainly exist. But Galveston's paradisiacal status stems from more than mere aesthetics. In less than two hundred years and a handful of generations, island city inhabitants have managed to forge a legacy of endurance through their far-reaching vision and a remarkable, indefatigable spirit of hope.

That legacy has been traced and combed through and retold countless times. Some look for it in the stoic Victorian buildings, others search for it in documents and manuscripts. But one can only truly witness the magnificence of island history through the eyes of the ones who lived it, the people whose life stories weave together to write the tale of an unsinkable island.

Of course the most well-known of these stories typically feature entrepreneurs, philanthropists, ingenious businessmen and builders of empires, many of whom are local icons even if they did not always achieve their success by what most would consider legitimate means. Less known, however, is another select group who similarly managed to forgo societal expectations and elevate themselves into the upper echelon of Galveston's once-rampant underground. This particular group was comprised of women who were living at a time when their options were severely limited. They had only one thing to sell, but they knew the law of supply and demand; as far as they were concerned, that was the only law that mattered.

And Galveston was ready for them. Surrounded by the sea and thus unfettered by trivialities like rules and regulations or regard for any outsider's opinion, an island in the Gulf of Mexico had assembled a backdrop against which the oppressed and repressed would find power and prestige or, at the very least, infamy and independence.

WALL STREET OF THE SOUTH

Galveston's location and natural harbor were first recognized as a viable port by the pirate Jean Lafitte in the early 1800s, but his occupation of the island lasted only four years. In 1821, he was forced off of Galveston Island by the United States Navy, which was acting under an alliance with Mexico, the official landlord of the Texas territory at the time. From that point, it was used sparingly as a Mexican trading post until Michel B. Menard secured permission from the Mexican government to establish a colony there in 1833.

Menard purchased a parcel of land located toward the eastern end of the island, atop the point of its highest elevation and bordering its northern edge along the harbor. In 1838, two years after Texas gained its independence from Mexico, Galveston was officially incorporated as a city and commerce immediately began to thrive. Growth of the port was steady and rose even more sharply after the annexation of Texas into the

United States in 1845, but the upward climb was violently interrupted by the onset of the Civil War in 1861, during which residents of the city cleared out to make way for the port to be occupied at varying times by both Union and Confederate soldiers.

When fighting finally ceased and the Federal blockade was lifted in 1865, Galveston seemed to make up for lost time, spurred on by a postwar cotton boom and the port's advantageous location that placed it closer to the goods of the West and Midwest than any other Gulf port by nearly five hundred miles. Within fifteen years, Galveston was the largest city in Texas, and its economy was exchanging nearly $40 million per year. One block away from the harbor was Strand Street, the epicenter of the downtown commercial district, which was doing its best to keep up with the port. The increase in imports and exports spawned the need for banks to handle the quickly amassing capital and insurance to protect valuable assets. One by one, the modest wooden commercial buildings lining the Strand were replaced with towering three- and four-story brick structures built by preeminent Victorian architects, and soon after the street earned a national reputation as the "Wall Street of the South." By the end of the nineteenth century, Galveston's populace had become so prosperous that it ranked among the wealthiest cities in the nation and even hosted an unofficial mansion-building contest along the island's main thoroughfare, Broadway Avenue.

In addition to a flourishing international port of commerce, Galveston was in possession of a port of immigration that once logged more names on its incoming registry than Ellis Island. This resulted in what was by far the most unique aspect of Galveston's rise to prominence: the creation of an open-minded and diverse culture among its residents. While the rest of the world was bogged down in adhering to a strict Victorian code of ethics inspired by the reign of Great Britain's most virtuous of monarchs, the port of Galveston found itself more than willing to accommodate a vast array of international personalities who were oblivious to such formalities. This resulted in a tolerant (although still well-defined) class structure, as well as an eagerness to embrace customs from all over the world. Aided also by the city's formation as a "walking town" in which the residential areas represented a broad spectrum of incomes and were not necessarily arranged by class, Galveston both attracted and served to incubate a community of acceptance.

Octopus of the Gulf

The first half of 1900 produced every indication that it was going to be a banner year for the island city; the growth of the port was seemingly unstoppable, and Galveston's population was the highest it had ever been. The second half was a different story altogether. On September 7, a storm that today would be considered a Category 4 hurricane struck an unprepared and unsuspecting island. The Great Storm of 1900 wiped two-thirds of the island clean and still stands as the deadliest natural disaster to ever hit U.S. soil, claiming a documented six thousand lives, although historians believe the actual number of casualties was between eight and ten thousand. But while some people and communities would view this as an insurmountable tragedy, Galveston rallied with historic vigilance and rose from the proverbial ashes stronger than ever.

Prominent citizen Ike Kempner recognized an opportunity in the dismantled leadership of a town in complete disarray and set about to restructure the city management to a never before utilized commission form of government that resembled a board of directors. A ceremonial mayor and five commissioners, each overseeing a specific facet of city operations, was such a novel and progressive idea that it was soon adopted by several other cities across the state and around the country. It granted Kempner and his allies nearly autonomous control over the defunct city government, and in their capable and well-meaning hands the transition soon resulted in a balanced ledger and large-scale improvements, though the success of the new system made the voting population rather blind to the system's potential for corruption if it were to fall in the wrong hands.

Under this new regime, a once-bankrupt Galveston was able to fortify its islandic perch by way of a marvelously decadent civil engineering project that constructed a two-mile long, seventeen-foot-high seawall along the Gulf side and elevated the southern half of the island by an average of thirteen feet. Meanwhile on the port side, the destruction had made way for fantastic improvements, including a sixty-acre wharf that could dock nearly one hundred vessels. To put it to work, interested parties and city officials shamelessly campaigned their resources across the entire western half of the United States and created so many exportation arms into the nation's interior that envious onlookers gave it the nickname the "Octopus of the Gulf."

Despite the name's malevolent underpinnings, Galveston wore it as a badge of honor, as proof of its ferocious tenacity and a statement of its uncanny ability to conjure a grotesque level of prosperity from the bowels of abject horror. The success also helped to revive the sense of invincibility that was prevalent in the island community prior to the 1900 storm, especially after several national news outlets covered the destruction and speculated that the city would never be rebuilt. The island had again proclaimed itself untouchable, and its defiance of Mother Nature would make it easy for it to challenge another opponent that was less powerful but equally foreboding: the federal government.

PLAYGROUND OF THE SOUTHWEST

Galveston's port and those involved saw no end to their ability to accrue lucrative components of the nation's shipping industry. Fifty miles to the north, city officials in Houston had been prattling on for decades about dredging a waterway from the Gulf up into the center of the city, but with a glaring absence of organized and motivated leaders, the prospect seemed highly unlikely. Until, of course, it happened. In 1914, President Woodrow Wilson officially opened the Houston Ship Channel; this immediately halted Galveston's sovereignty over the Gulf.

Fortunately for the city, the seawall that was built merely for protective purposes had unpredictably become an economic asset as well. Engineers who surveyed Galveston after the storm in preparation for the wall's construction and the grade-raising specifically planned for the two hundred feet directly behind the seawall to be elevated to the same height. This expanse soon became known as Seawall Boulevard, and although Houston had stripped Galveston of its commercial title, the humbled island city now found itself regally designated "Treasure Island" and the "Playground of the Southwest."

Although becoming a resort town had never really been part of the plan, Galveston embraced its new identity and proceeded full throttle. Construction along the seawall exploded as luxury accommodations, modern bathhouses and dazzling spectacles such as Electric Park established Galveston once again as the first city of its kind in Texas. Then, in 1920, the federal government passed Prohibition. But outlawing alcohol was no deterrent against two men who were destined to be outlaws themselves.

Free State of Galveston

Galveston County had been dry since 1918, a policy enacted as a show of support for the ongoing nationwide prohibition movement. Not coincidentally, that was the same year that Broadway Avenue became the dividing line between the turfs of two local gangs. The Beach Gang controlled the area south of the avenue, and the Downtown Gang presided over the north side; both were working to fill the supply gap left by the legislated illegality of alcohol. The Beach Gang soon stumbled upon a pair of business partners just arrived from Sicily. Both brothers and barbers, Sam and Rose Maceo worked chairs at the Galvez Hotel and Murdoch's Bathhouse on the seawall. Beach Gang leaders Ollie Quinn and Dutch Voight colluded with the Maceos to ply their barbershop customers with free samples of bootlegger's best, presuming with near certainty that they would come back for more.

The scheme worked, demand skyrocketed and Sam and Rose found themselves poised to expand their enterprises. Gambling seemed like the most natural choice. After all, the local community had a long history of doing as it pleased and making its own rules, and judging by the exponential increase in its current services with virtually no interference by law enforcement, city officials seemed to have no problem abiding by the same, self-made code. The brothers purchased property on the Gulf side of Seawall Boulevard at Twenty-First Street and established their first casino disguised as a restaurant, but by the late 1920s, the Grotto had already been forcibly shut down by the Texas Rangers. However, the Maceos were undeterred by these events, especially considering that the same whirlwind of state-sanctioned crackdowns had also conveniently removed the leaders of both local gangs and left the Maceos the sole proprietors of Galveston vice.

Sam and Rose singlehandedly perpetuated Galveston's success as a resort destination for nearly forty years. Not only did the draw of their alternative entertainment practically print money for the island's hotel and restaurant industry, as well as anyone directly or indirectly involved in hospitality, it also translated into currency for locals who still found themselves gainfully employed and peacefully sequestered while the rest of the nation faced the agonies of the Great Depression and World War II. Most importantly, Sam had the foresight to realize that his underground operations depended quite heavily on Galveston's aboveboard reputation. He was tireless in his promotion of the island

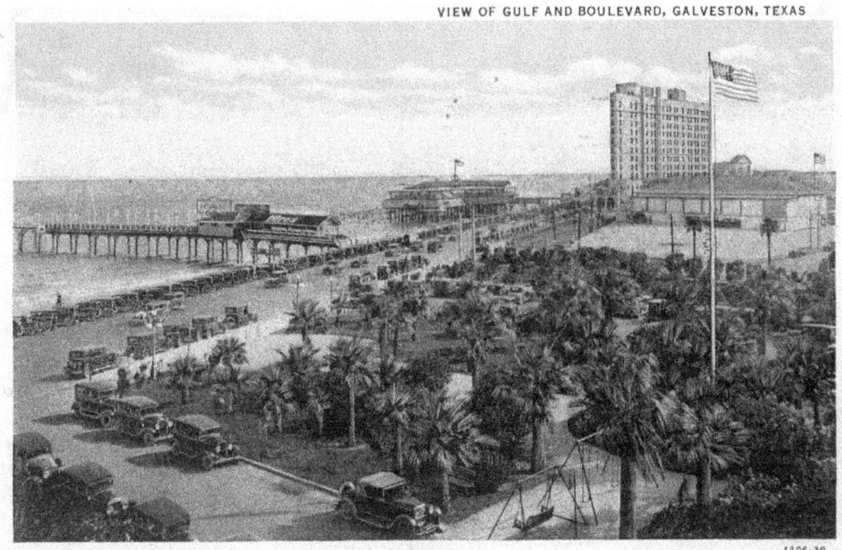

A 1934 postcard with a view from the Hotel Galvez shows the Maceos' original over-the-water location that would eventually become the world-famous Balinese Room. *Author's personal collection.*

and the Maceo establishments, utilizing his debonair charm to dazzle radio listeners and television watchers and convince celebrities to make appearances and perform at his clubs. He formed the Galveston Beach Association, wherein was formulated a marketing scheme that included a massive launch party and a bathing beauties pageant for the start of the summer season. His strategies would garner the island international attention for decades.

Sam died in 1951. Rose followed soon after in 1954. In 1955, the heirs to the underground, the Maceos' nephews Vic and Anthony Fertitta, unwittingly made a national mockery of Texas law enforcement when they attacked a reporter from a national magazine in the lobby of the Galvez. Less than two years later, Texas elected attorney general Will Wilson, who ran on a platform that centered on his draconian desire to clean up Galveston whatever the cost. Irreparably damaged by the loss of the Maceos' leadership, the previously impenetrable Free State of Galveston appeared to succumb to Wilson's ruthless yet mysterious vendetta. Widely praised and even reelected, history reveals that his tactics were superficial, and so were his results. Galveston would be done when Galveston said it was done, and not a minute sooner.

Part I

The District

1
IN THE BEGINNING

Prostitution needs no introduction. Its origins cannot even be effectively traced, because it has always existed, although its inception was most likely inspired by desperation. Only within the last one or two centuries has the point of human existence been about anything more than survival; until relatively recently, mankind's only real goal was to stay alive. At some point, that survival required a woman to have currency or, at the very least, something with which to barter. She did not have either of those, but she did have a service she could provide.

On the other hand, society's reaction to prostitution is rather accurately documented. Much like high fashion, with its shape-shifting style palette that sweeps through civilized societies the world over, the oldest profession has also demonstrated trends over time, be it an uptick in efforts to curtail it, periods of general acceptance and even the way it was organized within city limits. The most recognizable and longest standing of these trends was the formation of segregated districts. Long before its connation was most closely identified with racial strife in the 1960s, the term "segregation" almost exclusively referred to the distinct separation of bawdy house districts from the rest of the respectable public. This linguistic idiosyncrasy utterly voids any plausible deniability of the universal acceptance of the sex trade during the time it was used, yet the majority of the designated vice zones operated only on a de facto basis, and prostitution was rarely legalized outright.

The earliest recorded practice of confining prostitutes to certain streets dates to eleventh-century India in the city of Dhara,[1] thus it was not at all an uncommon concept by the time the United States was founded and American cities began to take root. However, the inclusion of segregated districts was never a strategic part of urban planning; rather, it always appeared to be a natural progression, the result of a seemingly inevitable demographic shift that occurred in cities tolerant of prostitution. Galveston's red-light district did not fully take shape until the 1890s, even though the city had prostitutes from its beginning in the 1830s,[2] and history predating the city's existence takes its presence back even further to the island's first nonnative resident.

Once a lauded privateer and the personal weapon of several European governments in their quest for naval dominance, the pirate Jean Lafitte had been effectively banished and was hiding out in New Orleans in the 1800s when he heard about Galveston Island. He quickly adopted it as his unofficial headquarters, undeterred by the fact that it was inhabited by a tribe of Karankawa—especially considering that among the native people were beautiful women willing to accept Lafitte and his men's offerings of extravagant gifts in exchange for companionship. However, the famed pirate apparently went too far when he successfully recruited their most beautiful maiden; a band of Karankawa warriors unleashed on Lafitte's camp, and legend recalls that two hundred of his men battled for an entire day to fend them off.[3]

Geographically and economically, the city of Galveston was founded along the northern bayside of the island, where nature had created a splendid harbor followed promptly by man's addition of a commercial port. Not coincidentally, the first prostitutes in Galveston established themselves above and around the saloons located near the wharves and port facilities on Water Street (today Avenue A/Harborside Drive). The most notable peddler of promiscuity during the port's early days was a man named Monroe Edwards. He had rightly earned an audacious reputation as a conman and a forger as well as a slave trader, which he then augmented by opening a number of locations in Galveston and Anahuac that offered gambling, whiskey and women.[4]

Five blocks away, Postoffice Street (Avenue E) had become one of the most fashionable residential streets during Galveston's prewar days, flanked on both sides by exquisite houses and the swanky summer homes of cotton planters.[5] When war broke out between the states, the city found itself plucked from a hopeful commercial future and transformed into a military outpost. Since it was the closest port to Mexico, an ally of the Union, the island's role was crucial in supplying a lifeline of resources to inland troops. Unfortunately for its residents, this induced a very real fear that military occupation could invite massive destruction of property or worse, confiscation by the federal government in the case of a takeover by Union troops. The majority of islanders fled; many of them also scrambled to sell their properties.

The Union did in fact wrest control of the island on October 15, 1862, but less than three months later, the Confederacy launched a surprise attack in the early hours of New Year's Day 1863 and reclaimed control. Despite this brief occupation, the Union still managed to find enough time to completely restructure the section of Postoffice Street closest to the port, east of Twenty-Fifth Street. This transition, coupled with the mass evacuation of homeowners, led to a stark devaluation of the residential properties along the outlying parts of Postoffice west of Twenty-Fifth Street. While most people saw it logical to move out of Galveston during the war, one particular group of tradeswomen thought it wiser to move in. They were of a select group adept at calculating the exchange rate of hundreds of bored, lonely and cash-rich soldiers.[6]

Very little of the damage sustained by Galveston during the war was lasting; months into Reconstruction, little evidence of it remained. By far, the most tangible imprint of wartime on the city was the way it directly impacted the cityscape to make way for a red-light district. Because of the commercialization of Postoffice Street, a five-block stretch of enormous homes with numerous bedrooms, located close enough to the port and commercial district to be accessible but far enough away to be discreet, was abandoned and rendered worthless to almost everyone except a current or aspiring madam. During the last half of the war and into Reconstruction, ambitious prostitutes from the port and a number of well-established madams from New Orleans ravaged the cheap real estate[7] and unknowingly started a phenomenon that would last nearly a century. Saloons, bars and even barbers soon followed the captive audience, and suddenly an abandoned street had become one of the liveliest and unruliest areas of town.

Public sentiment regarding the area at the time was one of abject denial, as indicated by the aftermath of an article published in 1866 in a Galveston periodical, *Flake's Daily Bulletin*. In "A Night with the Demi-Monde," a reporter claimed that several high-profile leaders of the city and local churches had been entertained at a gathering hosted by Miss Vic Morton. It was a raucous event whose hostesses were clad in various stages of undress from ballet costumes and robes to knee-high pants and ball gowns, an obvious revelation of the intent of the party despite the invitations suggesting that it was a distinguished occasion. But rather than lashing out at the hostess or the event itself, public outrage was expressly directed at the reporter. They attacked his character and even went so far as to accuse him of plagiarizing a burlesque play.[8]

Residents also chose to look the other way even after a rather highly publicized encounter ended in murder. A certain Major Anderson of the Union army who was stationed in Galveston during Reconstruction had taken up for the night in one of his favorite houses. A prostitute named Marie was cozily snuggled up on the major's lap when a young man named Bud Cotton barged into the room. A member of one of Galveston's high-society families who also happened to be smitten with Marie, Bud was liquored up and already in a mean humor, soon exacerbated by the discovery of his love in the arms of a Yankee. He threw Marie to the floor violently and then deftly disemboweled the major with a hawkbill knife.

Bud was tried by the Union and sentenced to hang, and after several rejected appeals, his fate was certain when Marie visited him in his cell the night before his execution. Witnesses claim she stood at the cell door and pulled him close, then whispered something in his ear and kissed him through the metal bars. The next morning, when soldiers came to retrieve Bud for his scheduled punishment, he was dead. No one ever quite figured out if she slipped him a vial or poisoned him herself with that last kiss, but as far as the Unionists were concerned, the debt was paid and the case was closed.[9]

A small wave of reform did eke through during Reconstruction, but it was quickly squelched by a rather comical tale of serendipity. One of the premier madams of the Civil War and postwar era was named Cora Morris, a stunning beauty from Tennessee. She was graciously hosting a group of women from a local church who had called to try to persuade Miss Morris into purity, pleading with her to turn her life around and repent. Amid the platitudes and prayers spoken from the velvet couches of Cora's luxuriously styled parlor, a regular customer glided in through the front door as he had obviously done many times prior. They heard him cry from the hallway, "Hey, Cora, where's my baby, Helen?" right before he bounded into the parlor. There he found himself surrounded by a group of evangelical women who looked strangely familiar. Their identity was no longer a mystery after he looked over to see his wife faint into a crumpled heap on the floor.[10] After this incident, the respectable women of Galveston decided that the best way to deal with the issue was to politely ignore it.[11]

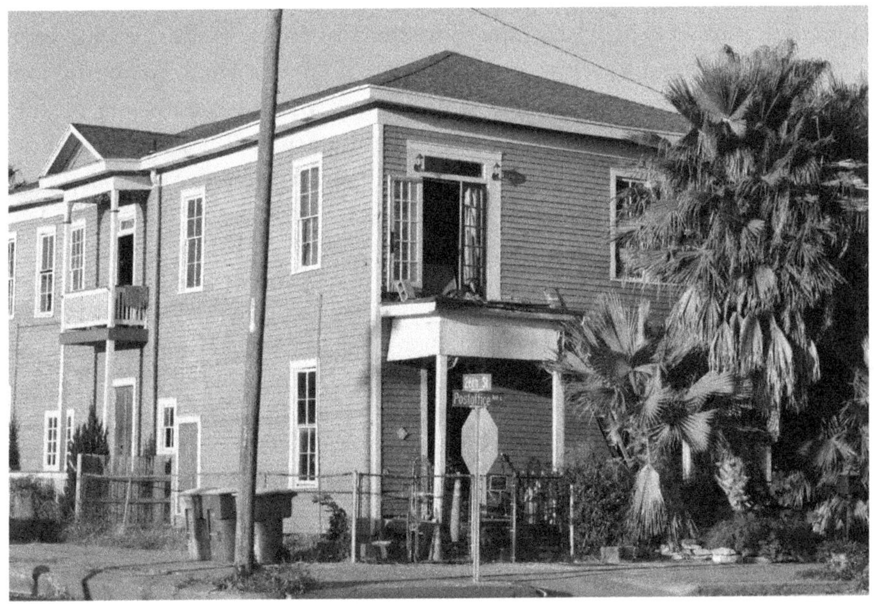

The 1886 house built by Mollie Waters at 2528 Postoffice. *Photo by author.*

By 1880, the proliferation of Galveston's seaport had likewise been accompanied by 489 saloons and as many as 55 brothels,[12] but it was not until 1886 that the Postoffice district truly began to make a name for itself when it received what would eventually become one of its most recognizable and longest-standing symbols. A woman named Mollie Waters, an outsider recently arrived to the island, had obtained several plots of land around the city. She chose from her purchases the northeast corner of Twenty-Sixth and Postoffice on which to build a massive, multi-roomed structure that she advertised as a female boardinghouse. The disguise was of course deceptive only to those who were not paying the slightest bit of attention, considering that the length of the house stretched over half of a block to accommodate an excessive number of upstairs bedrooms that all fed into one long hallway, and that it was built with entrances on both sides, one of which featured a screened-in porch that maintained visitors' anonymity.[13]

Not only did Mollie's architectural achievements indicate that she was a woman with a keen business sense, her upscale brothel complete with satin-clad ladies and an air of effortless sophistication also infused Postoffice Street with a sense of decorum comparable to honor among thieves. Her investments proved to be lucrative for the remainder of the district, and the street flourished in the years after her arrival as it gained a reputation as a "high-toned, well-regulated institution."[14] By the last decade of the nineteenth century, its popularity had finally earned it a nickname: The Line, a generic and obvious moniker that nevertheless firmly embedded prostitution onto the city's brand for decades to come.

2
HALCYON DAYS

During Galveston's most prosperous era, the rest of the globe battled an international economic depression sandwiched between two world wars. Until Prohibition, prostitution had been Galveston's only depravity, but the enterprising Maceo brothers were not hesitant to capitalize on people's desire for things they cannot have. After they expanded their business model into gambling, Galveston's triad of vice was complete. A city that fully maintained the notion of its own autonomy, coupled with a regular influx of thirsty consumers in the form of troops stationed at the military bases along the seawall, fueled a palpable sense of invincibility to which the ladies of the Line were certainly not immune.

At the turn of the twentieth century, Galveston's segregated district was on par with those of many other Texas cities in which prostitution had flourished alongside the economic heyday that accompanied the railroad boom of the 1880s and 1890s.[1] The railroad's link to prostitution is marked by the legend of how love for sale stumbled upon its most recognizable advertisement. Crews and engineers used red signal lights on the job, which also happened to be conveniently portable for carrying along with them when they ventured outside the railyard after dark. The sight of a red light on the porch of a house most likely began with the women who worked solo out of individual cribs, placed there by the visiting railroad worker to indicate she was occupied. But soon the look was adopted by savvy madams, and by the early 1900s, red lights had become a universal symbol of sex for hire.

Amid the proliferation of red-light districts across Texas, waves of resistance formed against their presence and general acceptance, steered by fervent church leaders and their auxiliary ladies groups, religious-minded politicians and incensed citizens. Prior to 1910, most of the protestations had been politely ignored and shoved aside before they were able to gain any real momentum, but between 1911 and 1915, the crusade became much more organized and succeeded in permanently closing the districts of Dallas, Austin and Amarillo while significantly undermining those of San Antonio and El Paso.[2]

Yet Galveston possessed something all of those towns did not—an audacious air of collective pride and entitlement, the result of the miraculous economic victory over the unspeakable tragedy of 1900, further inflamed by the completion of the mammoth seawall and grade-raising projects.[3] Many of the women on the Line had witnessed both the destruction and the rebuilding as closely as any resident had, and they shared an innate distrust of outsiders who were unable to empathize with their experiences. Although this sense of commonality was much too sentimental for city officials, they did have a desire to remove prostitutes from the beachfront and place them out of sight from tourists and the soldiers of Fort Crockett. Galveston's red-light district was formally sanctioned by the city in 1910 and faced none of the scrutiny from residents that had arisen in the other parts of Texas.[4]

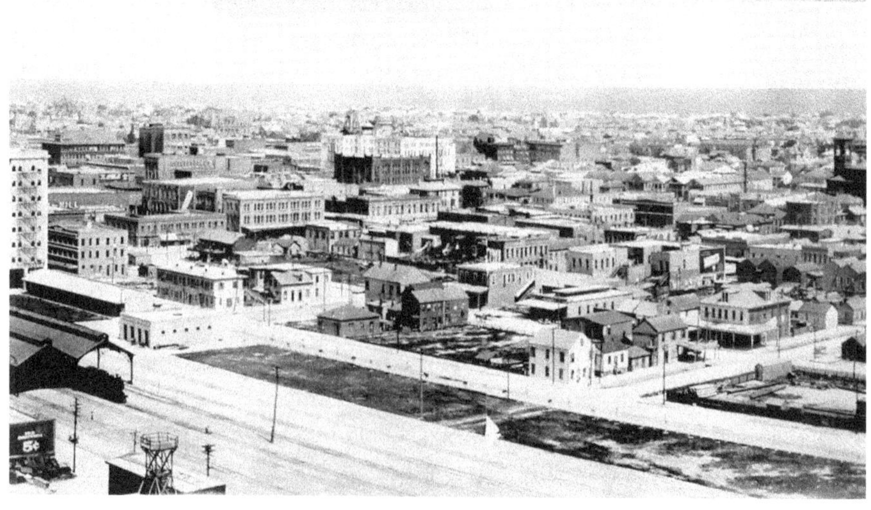

This 1915 panorama of downtown Galveston includes a section of the district (center right) that seamlessly blends in with the rest of the city. *Author's Personal Collection.*

Perhaps by the rest of the country's standards, the island's community was a bit unhinged, but its sense of self-sufficiency led to a widely held, practical and progressive conclusion that prostitution was a necessary evil, and the toleration of it allowed for more control and regulation than outright repression. Even a local Catholic bishop declared, "We segregate mental and physical disease, let's do the same for moral sickness, for soul sickness."[5] The people of Galveston were brimming with a spirit of independence and a subsequent "irritation [when] denied the right to determine their form of amusement."[6]

Thus the city carried on undaunted by outside opinion for several more years until World War I began and reformers across Texas discovered an unlikely alliance in the U.S. War Department. The Galveston Ministerial Association's crusade against local prostitution would last over forty years, and in 1917, its members took the first step toward aligning their cause with the federal government's. They sent a telegram to the secretary of war outlining the details of their unofficial survey of the situation. It read: "The Galveston Ministerial Association and patriotic citizens demand the protection of the uniform and the flag from 1,000 prostitutes within five miles and several saloons within a half mile of three companies of soldiers who buy liquor from bootleggers. The city is flooded with outcasts from other cities."[7]

The GMA's estimate was not far off, although it included prostitutes both within the district and others who worked either in the outlying areas or on their own in cribs around town. Near the start of World War I, police records indicated fifty houses operating within the district and thirteen questionable boardinghouses, with approximately ten to twelve girls per house. Those outside the district easily numbered several hundred.[8]

Galveston's city commissioners had hoped that their valiant attempt to corral prostitution within the bounds of the Postoffice Street district would be enough to pacify the U.S. government, but these same leaders were also cognizant of the primary concern, namely syphilis and the expense of its treatment, and humbly acquiesced when the army ordered the district be closed.[9] Interestingly, disease was always the one and only argument presented by the military when taking a stance against prostitution, which of course is directly related to its costliness; never was the practice itself officially rejected. Using this same logic in reverse would suggest that a lack of disease meant the extracurricular activities of soldiers were widely accepted internally, so long as the effects of it were not substantial enough to interfere with the army's public image.[10]

This explains why federal authorities issued a vociferous condemnation of Galveston's district at the start of the war that led to its "closure" but completely failed to actually enforce the nullification of prostitution despite common knowledge that the "For Rent" signs in the window were purely a farce and the back doors were always open. After being only temporarily satiated by the district being officially closed, the Ministerial Association soon discovered that its efforts had only served to scatter the working women across town, many of whom were now plying their trade along the beach. The chief of police claimed that his ineffectiveness in suppressing vice was directly caused by his inability to get military cooperation.[11]

Not surprisingly, when the war ended the military abruptly withdrew its support of the Ministerial Association, so members joined forces with other reformist organizations and turned next to the city commissioners to vie for support. Their pleas were ignored, and the district quickly regained its traction and returned to operating under the supervision of local police. In an attempt to at least thwart the spread of disease, a group of citizens did manage to persuade the city to implement a system that required the women to obtain regular inspections and health certificates. However, the system was corrupted in less than a year when the police officers in charge of the inspections were discovered to have been routinely accepting bribes for certificates. Instead of endeavoring to make improvements to the program, it was simply shut down.[12]

A more determined effort to eradicate the district from Galveston was made by Mayor W.A. Keenan in 1921 but fizzled after he became embroiled in a standoff over police policy with both the chief and commissioner of police. Keenan solicited twenty-five prominent citizens to serve on a committee dedicated to the elimination of vice; every single one of them declined to serve. The following year, another protest was organized by the Ministerial Association, but it only elicited a weak response from the city's panel of commissioners, who claimed they could not eliminate prostitution but would do their best to keep it to a minimum.[13]

This view held by city leaders in the 1920s was in tandem with that of the majority of Galveston residents, who also believed that removing prostitution was impossible and therefore controlling it was essential. A regulated district was also thought to undermine the potential for corruption in the police force; an open tolerance of the district theoretically meant that officers could not be paid off by madams to prevent raids or arrests, although in actuality many of them still chose to wield their power to produce cash for protection.[14] On the civilian side, one rather logical theory supposes that the public's general acceptance of the red-light district stemmed from Galveston's resort atmosphere.

William Roe was a brilliant promoter hired by the Maceos to market Galveston as a destination and resort town. Perhaps his most ingenious scheme was the invention of a beachside beauty contest that would eventually become the Miss Universe Pageant, but on a day-to-day basis Roe was most known for his persistent relationship with the local press. Of course the news he released was always positive, praising the merits of the town, its natural beauty and friendliness. This constant promotion of the city's merits in an attempt to aggrandize its appeal to out-of-town guests resulted in a "booster complex"—residents believed their own press, which most likely influenced the conversation among locals and possibly led to an inflated sense of superiority.[14]

The election of Mayor J.E. Pearce as Keenan's successor appears historically to have been yet another display of the city's standing, being that Pearce was quite satisfied with Galveston's solution of tolerance, whereas Keenan was not. However, during his term, Pearce maintained that the segregated district was never an issue of importance in any political race because the city had never really had much of a divide on its opinions of the issue. He was correct—news reports regarding Galveston's municipal campaigns had not mentioned the topic once in the fifteen years prior to Pearce's election. Constituents were much more concerned with the operation of the wharf and port, which was directly tied to an ongoing feud among three elite Galveston families. The relatively dramatic and high-profile conflict pitted the Moody family against the allied Kempner and Sealy families, none of whom wished to be seen as a supporter of vice, but neither did they care to be aligned with reformation. Since each faction supported opposing sides in any election, the matter of the city's relative indiscretions proved to be a nonstarter among those vying for city governance.[15]

The red-light district of Galveston thus carried on for nearly two more decades undisturbed. An educated estimate made in 1927 found that the number of prostitutes in Galveston had held steady since its last official estimate at the start of the war. The district contained fifty-four houses and another dozen suspiciously curious ones that for whatever reason could not be definitely determined to be bawdy houses.[16] Rather than sullying its reputation, the island was enjoying a regular influx of conventioneers from across the nation, and the lure of highly publicized events brought in crowds of staggering sizes to Seawall Boulevard, which only fed the belly of the Galveston underground. On the harbor side, the Port of

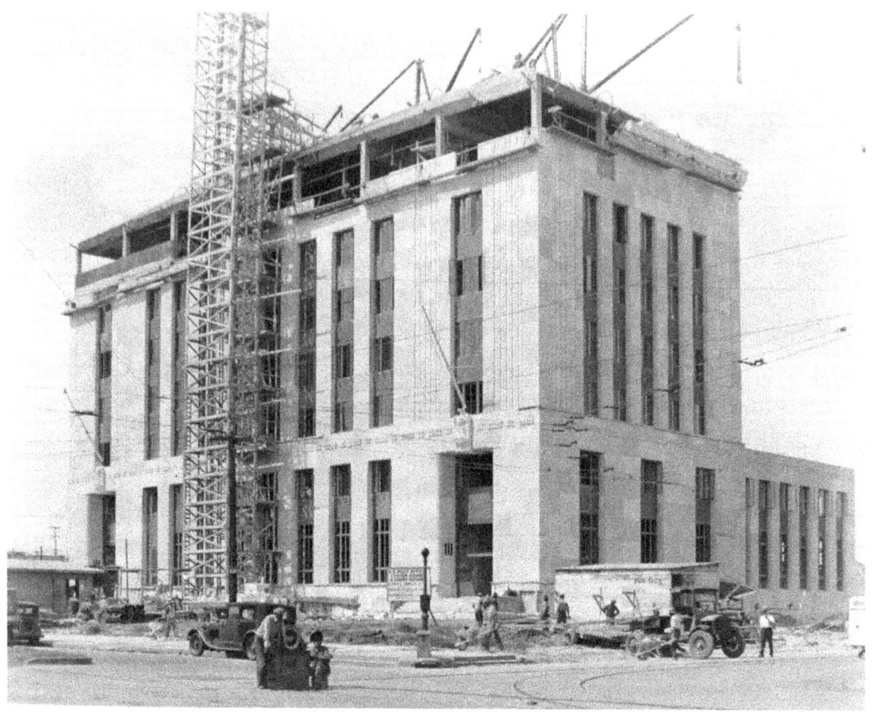

The 1934 construction of a combination customhouse, courthouse and post office located two blocks from the red-light district. *Courtesy of Rosenberg Library.*

Galveston was still the second largest export center in the United States and orchestrated up to thirty ships at any given time.[17] When the Great Depression seized the nation and most of the world with its paralyzing grip in 1929, the legitimate commerce kept the city's professional viability afloat while the well-established island economy of gambling, booze and love by the hour kept residents almost entirely sheltered and generally content.[18] As a subtle symbol of the city's continuing policy of tolerance, a massive new municipal building that combined a courthouse, customhouse and post office was built on Twenty-Fifth Street in 1934, two blocks away from the red-light district.

Meanwhile on Postoffice Street, the 1930s saw an influx of girls from all over the country who were looking to escape the miseries of the Depression experienced elsewhere, and the increased competition diminished the effect of Galveston's booming vice industry on the district. During the previous decade, houses on the Line had begun to show their first signs of aging, and few of them had occupants who were enough concerned with architectural aesthetics to keep the situation from worsening. Now that the red-light district had a supply that was outpacing even the exaggerated demand, and also because it was subject to outside interference much more so than the gambling or illegal liquor businesses that were squarely in the hands of the Maceos, Postoffice was fast losing its luster. Low-end houses with cut-rate prices began to creep in and multiply, slowly choking out the few remnants of glitz from the late nineteenth and early twentieth centuries. Further removing the district's glamour of yore were the cheap hawking practices of the modern houses. Gone were the days of girls being sought after in their elegant boudoirs by discreet gentlemen; rivalry along the Line had now forced them to post up on balconies and hang out of upper-floor windows in shorty pajamas to lure passersby.[19]

The saturated district received a reprieve as the entrance of a new decade slowly lifted the fog of recession from the United States, and it was further bolstered by the start of a new war, which presented new opportunities to women and subsequently steadied the Line's supply. Galveston was again the temporary home to ten thousand military personnel every month, meaning that Postoffice Street again became a target of the federal government. The red-light district was officially closed by the army for a second time, but, just as before, only the completely uninformed would be

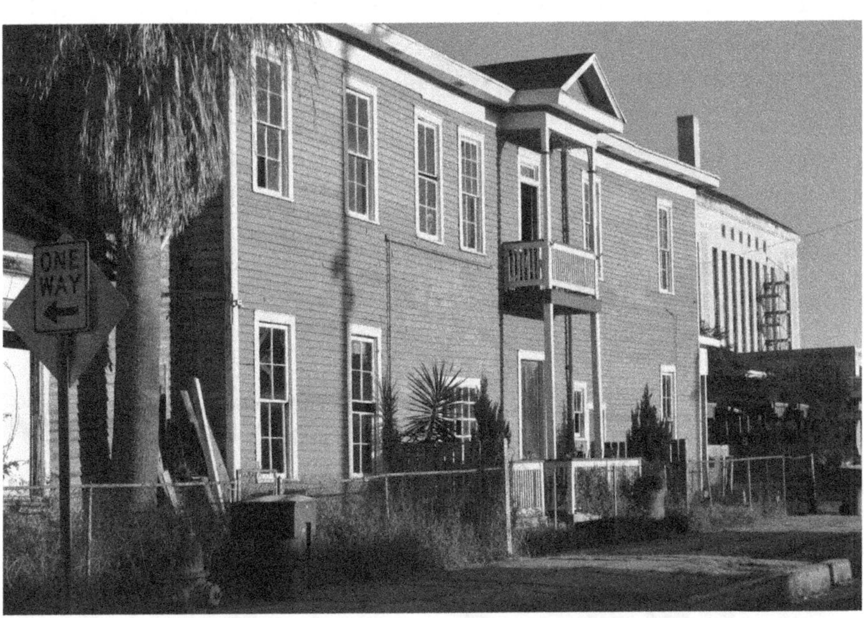

The Twenty-Sixth Street view of Mother Harvey's bordello at 2528 Postoffice includes the 1934 Customs House in the background and its proximity to the district. *Photo by author.*

fooled by the view from the street and unaware that a girl was waiting for him at the back door. They also found as the war went on that Galveston's tolerance had not waned and that city officials were altogether uninterested in shutting the houses down completely.[20]

In 1943, eleven houses that operated on a "lavish" scale and "a myriad of less pretentious ones" were said to be operating in the district, but its official closure had also scattered many other women to areas all around the city. The police department did make a good show of attempting to suppress prostitution to the public by issuing frequent orders to raid houses and printing the results of each in the newspaper, but it was described by one journalist as "almost like trying to hold water in a sieve."[21] The press continued to survey the situation optimistically throughout the war, reporting on the police chief's regular raids and speculating that prostitution was obviously declining when one of the raids only netted five women.[22] As the war came to an end, local reformers published declarations that residents should remain diligent so that the "gains" made during the conflict should not be lost.[23]

Somehow the originators of these optimistic reports were oblivious to the fact that during the 1940s, the Line represented an industry that, aside from the girls, employed nearly one thousand people in the city, or 2 percent of the population.[24] It had outwitted the U.S. military and the local press, but the red-light district of Galveston had yet to meet its most formidable opponent.

3

AN ISLAND INQUISITION

During World War II, men and women across the country answered the call of their patriotic duty. The men went to war, and the women went to work. The doors of opportunity were blown open, as employment that had always been off-limits to the "fairer" sex was readily available now that their male counterparts were battling in the literal trenches of Europe. The role of worker and wage earner was one American women accepted most readily, which meant that when the war ended, they were not altogether content to return to their former lifestyles. Those who chose to remain employed accounted for one-third of the postwar labor force in the United States.

Despite these numbers, or perhaps because of them, the powers that be thought it wiser on a grand scale to again relegate women to the lingering Victorian ideals of home and family, referred to as the culture (or cult) of domesticity. Also known as the cult of true womanhood, this value system placed emphasis on piety, purity, domestic achievements and submission. After the war, mass media proved to be a powerful tool for the dissemination of this female archetype, aided even more by the spread of television, and these were fully exploited in an attempt to convince women of their place. Print ads in national magazines lauded the "respectable" woman who maintained an efficient household and provided a nurturing environment for her husband, a concept later perpetuated by the launch of television sitcoms in the 1950s that encapsulated this model, such as *Leave It to Beaver*, *Father Knows Best* and

The Donna Reed Show. Marriage rates and home ownership skyrocketed with the idyllic notion of the American Dream.

The rise of Communism and the Cold War that began in the late 1940s further exacerbated the manufactured need for these standards, as the pronouncement of the United States as a Christian nation fueled by family values was used to set it aloft of other nations. This mindset eventually led to the addition of "Under God" to the pledge of allegiance in 1954 and a joint resolution of Congress in 1956 that required the placement of "In God We Trust" on American currency. Although well intended, this push for a set of ideals not shared by the entirety of the populace led to a countermovement of discontent toward the reestablishment of these principles in a country that was ultimately meant to be a beacon of diversity and nonconformity. Galveston of course did not intend to be a symbol of this discontent, but its fierce sense of isolation and independence certainly made it one in hindsight.

Throughout the rest of Texas, cities appeared willing to subscribe to this re-invented morality, and openly tolerated vice districts more or less vanished. Even though levels of prostitution exhibited an upswing after wartime repression lifted, cribs and bawdy houses were abandoned elsewhere in Texas, and prostitutes typically worked out of hotels.[1] Such was not the case in Galveston, where the city made its first postwar declaration of its intention to continue on as it saw fit by electing Herbert Cartwright as mayor. He would go on to serve four terms from 1947 until 1955. Cartwright and his supporters, many of whom were the upper echelon of the underground, wanted the city wide open. The rest of the city seemed to want it, too, as most of them were aware of the positive impact that tolerance had on the local economy.[2]

History tells little of how exactly the Galveston elites regarded prostitution specifically within the web of vice, other than what can be assumed by the awareness of particular ladies' church groups. They did not openly protest against the segregated district but seemed to regard Galveston as a hotbed of temptation for young women and often sought to discourage them from staying in the city.[3] If Postoffice Street itself was any indication, it pointed in the other direction. Cars were piled up curbside all hours of the day and night,[4] and even local teenagers were fascinated by the Line's presence. Young women would ask their dates to drive them down to the Line so they could see it for themselves, although many times they would duck down and hide so as not to be seen in such an unscrupulous area.[5] Local politicians, on the other hand, would flaunt the district to visiting executives and use the prowess of the young women to sway them to move their business headquarters to the island.

Galveston vice received its first major blowback in 1951, when the Crime Commission of the Texas legislature launched a full-scale probe into the island underground. Mayor Cartwright and seventeen other local officials were called to Austin to testify; cower under the strong arm of Texas law they did not. When the presiding judge asked the mayor for his advice on what the committee should recommend to the legislature, he answered, "Regulated prostitution, liquor by the drink, and gambling." This was after asserting with the most heartfelt conviction that breaking state law was unquestionably acceptable for Galveston because it was Texas's unofficial playground.[6] Later, he balked, "If God couldn't stop prostitution, then why should I try?"[7] But these were merely diversions on the mayor's part. The state was less concerned with the bawdy babes of Postoffice than it was with the two-ton truck full of Maceos' accounting records that had been brought into Austin.[8] The real object of its investigation was the revelation of a $2.8 million profit from a $3.5 million gross for the year 1950, which implies that the legislature's issue was not necessarily how the money was being made but that it was being made in a way that denied the state its fair share.[9]

Yet waiting in the wings was an organization that was all too happy to pick up the slack of the Crime Commission on the issue of prostitution. The American Social Hygiene Association[10] was founded in 1914 as part of the social hygiene movement, an offshoot of the social purity movement (circa 1860–1910), whose singular goal was to abolish prostitution and other sexual immoralities as defined by the tenets of the Christian faith. Although the modern version was marketed to aim more at sexual education and the control of venereal disease, its underpinnings were identical, and prostitution was still its focus. A chapter of the ASHA had been assigned to Galveston since 1944, when it began conducting undercover surveys of the red-light district. The surveys measured the size of the community, the number of prostitutes found through covert investigations and the "flagrancy with which it is conducted."[11]

Granted, the association was well aware of the challenges it faced. Field investigators regularly reported of Galveston's island habitat and the "psychology of isolation" as a factor in the city's stern disregard for outside influence,[12] as well as the fact that corruption seemed to be ingrained in the city.[13] But by 1949, the ASHA had collected enough data against Galveston to devise a concrete plan of action. It would provoke public opinion through church and community groups, and once enough support was obtained,

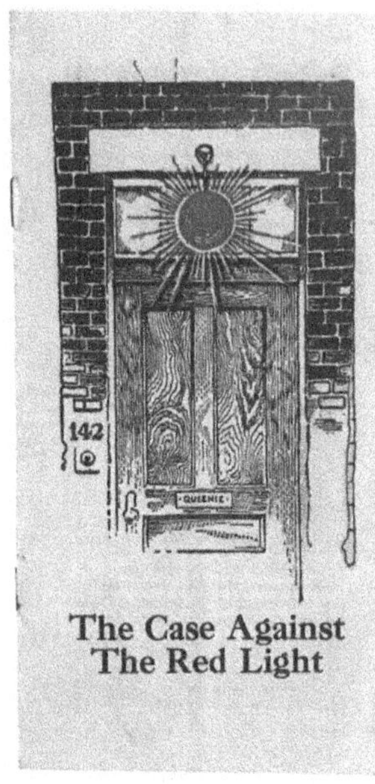

"The Case against the Red Light" from 1923 is an example of the literature disseminated by reform groups in the early to mid-twentieth century. *Author's personal collection.*

it would coordinate with the army to make a demand to the city commissioners.[14] After recruiting the support of the Galveston Ministerial Association and other civic and church groups, the ASHA launched its campaign. It distributed informational pamphlets around the city and organized meetings at which its representatives would speak on the "High Calling of Parenthood" and Family Life Education.[15]

The general public of Galveston ignored the ASHA for years, but it was organized, efficient and most of all possessed a level of tenacity that would have been commendable if it had not been so ultimately destructive. In 1953, almost a decade since beginning investigations into the underbelly of Galveston, the association found itself exasperated and angry after it was promised and then denied assistance from the Texas attorney general at the time, John Ben Sheppard (1953–57). Then, in an ironic twist, the ASHA took a page out of Galveston's tip book and decided to face disappointment head-on. The group concluded that it did not in fact need permission from the government—city lawmakers had long since been hopeless, and now the state's were equally so. The association decided to do it itself, without sanction or authorization—and that made them much more like the people of Galveston than they would ever admit.

The association's dedicated representatives, adjuncts and volunteers spent the first part of 1953 on the next phase of their crusade. Inspired by the slow but steady growth of its influence, the ASHA created a Citizens Committee for the express purpose of presenting an official petition to the state government to obtain injunctions and padlock houses. In order for the scheme to work, they would need ten thousand signatures, an enormous undertaking. Thus the ASHA regional representative assigned to Galveston at the time, Howard Slutes, planned a visit to Austin to see Attorney General Sheppard for insurance purposes. If the petition was successful, it would be underwritten by a promise of cooperation from Sheppard; if it was not, they would still have the assurance of his backing. Slutes was well received and promised full support on his first visit, but when a follow-up visit was made shortly after, Sheppard outright refused audience. This stunned Slutes until a few days later, when the Texas governor made a speech to the East Texas Police Officers Association and emphasized how important it was for the state to stay out of local law enforcement issues. He also smugly implied that any city should only enforce the rules it cared to enforce. Slutes openly assumed that the governor's office had played a large part in Sheppard's relinquishment of his promise.[16]

Perhaps as a token of repentance, Sheppard sent two lawyers from his office to Galveston to file restraining orders and injunctions against three houses in the district. The ASHA responded not with gratitude but with a glorified sense of purpose that resulted in an audacious but effective move. James Bradner, a junior owner at Galveston radio station KGBC, visited the owners of six different houses on the Line and told them that they would be publicly humiliated if injunctions should be placed against them, and that the only reason the owners had this warning was because Bradner himself had asked for time to notify his "friends." It was an act that even a Galvestonian could appreciate, and all six owners bought it hook, line and sinner. They evicted their tenants, who scattered to cheap hotels.[17]

The group was given no chance to gloat, however. To the extreme embarrassment of the committee, Commissioner of Police Walter Johnston announced that the district was closed mere hours after the ASHA had rendered the houses padlocked and shut down. This in turn prompted Sheppard's office to refuse any further assistance, since the problem had obviously been solved.[18] The association's success was also fleeting because it was ultimately ineffective—it had closed the red-light district but had not eliminated prostitution. In fact, five months after the district was closed, conditions were deemed so bad that Judge Donald Markle of the Tenth District ordered a grand jury investigation into Galveston prostitution.[19] One year later, the county attorney announced that a prostitution ring had been uncovered by way of three raids that resulted in thirteen arrests.[20]

Another glaring downside to abolishing the district, especially while prostitution was still tolerated by residents, was that it resulted in extreme corruption within the police department. Commissioner Johnston and many of his officers were actually profiting from desegregation and frequently collected payoffs from madams and girls who needed protection now that their trade was "officially" frowned upon. One particular owner admitted in court to paying Johnston $200 per month for every house of prostitution he owned,[21] and at one point in the mid-1950s, Johnston was speculated to have raked in $40,000 throughout the course of his term.[22] To account for what seemed like a lack of action on his part, since few arrests were being made, he explained that he was happy to raid a house if it was pointed out to him, but his salary did not include playing investigator to look for brothels.[23]

Roy Clough, a candidate for mayor in the spring of 1955, had grown particularly weary of Johnston's corrupt operations. On the day he was elected, Clough announced that he planned to reopen the district and bring gambling back out into the open, and by Galveston standards his reasoning was quite sound. Besides maintaining the stock argument that vice was an economic necessity to the city, publicly he was most keenly focused on the degradation of conditions in Galveston since the red-light district had been closed. The prostitutes had not left, they had only moved to seedy hotels and now solicited people on the street and in bars.[24] Taverns were "lousy" with them, Clough said in his usual colorful manner. Privately, Clough argued that if anyone should be making money off the prostitutes, it should be the city and not a commissioner. By reestablishing tolerance for the district, raids would be increased substantially and fines would be paid to the city rather than bribes to the policemen.[25]

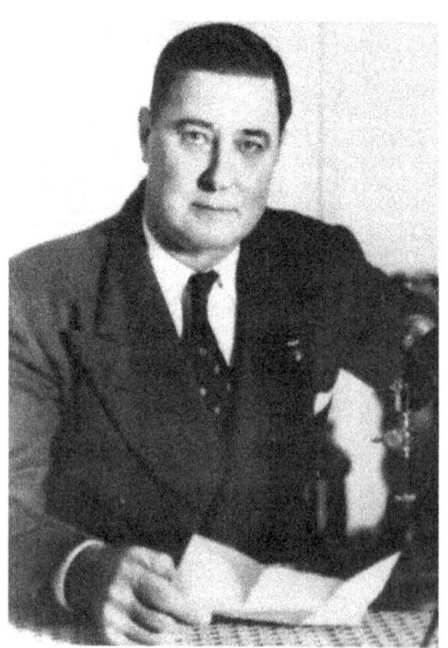

Roy Clough was elected mayor of Galveston in 1955 and immediately received national attention for his plan to reopen the segregated district. *Author's personal collection.*

Clough's bold statements and his brazen personality made him an instant national sensation, as magazines all over the country ran stories about the lunatic mayor and his wide-open city of sin. The attention to Clough was briefly interrupted in July 1955, when the ASHA released its most recent survey, which indicated eighteen bordellos were still in operation around the city. Commissioner Johnston, who had already publicly chastised Clough, allied with District Attorney Marsene Johnson, and together they gave the official order that all houses of prostitution close. Revealing the sincerity of his intentions, Clough responded that he was "tickled pink" at the announcement; if re-segregation was not an option, then prostitution should indeed be abolished.[26] Of course, Clough knew Johnston's insincerity, and unsurprisingly, his announcement produced little or no results in the long run.

The following month, the spotlight was again redirected from Clough when *Life* magazine published a scathing article, "Wide-Open Galveston Mocks Texas Laws." The articles about Clough had been almost whimsical and satirical, but then again they had been inspired by a flamboyant character and not an act of violence. Since both of the Maceos had passed away, the acceptance of vice by Galveston residents had been severely waning at the hands of their successors and cousins Vic and Anthony Fertitta. When one of them attacked a reporter in the lobby of the Hotel Galvez, it almost ruined them. The subsequent article, published in a national periodical, embarrassed islanders and raised a huge red flag to state officials.[27]

Clough ploughed ahead, however, perhaps content to draw some of the attention away from the Galvez incident. His most lengthy and stunning declarations were made in a chamber of commerce meeting in September 1955. He blasted Johnston, revealing that he was warning houses of raids to undermine the city's authority and of course to keep the payoffs for himself, and recounting a tale of a pimp refusing to pay a fine because he already paid Johnston. Despite Clough's rough-and-tumble personality and his willingness to insult the commissioner of police, his sincerity was apparent when he affirmed that he was "not a believer" in prostitution but he wanted it controlled for the good of the city. Again with sincerity, he pondered an ironic dilemma: the U.S. Army had informed him that it was not at all concerned with the amount of prostitutes in Galveston, but it still would not send vacationing troops to the island if the city had a recognized district. Lastly, Clough confronted the annoyance at all of the press he had received since his election, explaining that none of the publications had sought his approval.[28]

In October, he decided to confront the exaggerated and unapproved press by releasing his own statement to *Man's Magazine*.[29] Although punctuated by his trademark brusqueness and frank speech, the self-written article proved to be a feeble explanation of Galveston's reasoning for its choice of economy. The article did accomplish his end goal, but by a different means. Instead of convincing anyone of island logic, his tone removed all mystery and drama from the situation, and the press soon lost interest. With that issue out of the way, Clough returned his attention to making prostitution work for the city and not for Commissioner Johnston.

Two months into 1956, Clough was again front-page news, but this time only in Galveston. He announced that he was stepping up raids on houses to twice daily if necessary, remarking that he was more than willing to compensate for the "flagrant breakdown in law enforcement in Galveston due to the dereliction of the police commissioner."[30] Later in the year, after a daylight raid in May netted eight girls and six johns as well as a madam, Clough went so far as to act as the presiding judge at their arraignment, during which he denied the accused continuance but agreed to a jury trial; they were each released on a $200 bond. He also made it clear that he was willing to sit on the bench during the trials, but that was met with staunch opposition from the defense attorney.[31] Despite these antics, Clough was reelected in 1957, but the future of his city would prove to be entirely out of his hands.

In November 1956, reformers and the ASHA received their big break when Texas elected Will Wilson as its new attorney general. Described as a fearless man who adhered to a staunch moral code, he possessed an inordinate amount of disdain for Galveston. He claimed to believe in a strong local government, but he also felt it the duty of the state to intervene if local law enforcement was ineffectual. Upon his election, Wilson promised the people of Texas that he would remove the blight of island vice from the state by any means necessary, and he offered Galveston officials six months from when he took office in January to take care of it themselves.[32]

Those assigned to the Galveston chapter of the ASHA were immediately smitten and began corresponding with Wilson within days of the election. They sent him letters of praise and admiration and included their most recent surveys on prostitution. Publicly, Wilson had placed most of his emphasis on gambling, but the ASHA was determined to ensure that prostitution was also ensnared in his web of redemption. Over the course of the first half of 1957, Howard Slutes met often with Will Wilson; they discussed Galveston's potential as a family resort town and the impending difficulty of transitioning from a vice economy.[33]

All parties were highly optimistic and seemed to think that with all of the abundant resources on the island that make it a natural attraction, Galveston was in effect cutting off its nose to spite its face by its insistence on allowing vice conditions to remain. Yet Galveston residents simply refused to take Wilson's advice. They had no desire to turn their gritty and mysterious and raucous island into a tawdry family beach town. But the writing had been scribbled on the wall for years, ever since the Maceos died, and now their six months were up.

Wilson was like a man possessed on the bright summer day he decided to rain his wrath down on Galveston. His army of Texas Rangers were merciless as they broke down doors, smashed illegal liquor stashes and bashed in the faces of slot machines before loading them on a ship and dumping them into the middle of the harbor. He served every house on the ASHA's February list with permanent injunctions. He knew exactly where to go and when to be there—almost as if Galveston's six-month reprieve was actually just the time he needed to investigate, because somehow he knew that this unchained city would do nothing less than force his hand. And of course, he made sure the press was there to see it all. Across Texas, headlines regaled his honorable achievements. Wilson was a star while Galveston sat, battered and bruised, once again utterly lost within the depths of uninvited destruction.

The attorney general met with Mayor Clough and other city officials after the raids. Now that he had decided what was best for the city, he was more than willing to support them in any way he could to promote them as a tourist town and an industrial center. In a joint press conference, Clough agreed with Wilson on gambling but held his ground that prostitution would never be abolished and therefore should be regulated. "We've had [it] since the time of Christ," he declared adamantly, to which the pious Wilson responded that theft and murder have always existed, seemingly oblivious to his own incongruity regarding the resulting victimizations of those crimes. Toward the end of the conference, Wilson was asked if he hoped to receive as many votes from Galveston in the next election as he had in the last, to which he replied in the affirmative. Clough, always quick with a pithy last word, looked at the general and without missing a beat replied, "Mr. Wilson, would you like to make a bet?"[34]

Ultimately, Clough took the stance that he neither defended nor condemned Wilson's actions and maintained that he had nothing to do with the shutdown.[35] Regardless, he was defeated in the election of 1959 by none other than Herbert Cartwright, his predecessor, although it was speculated that he was elected only because of the public's disdain for Clough and not because of their desire to return to an open town.[36] But in reality, returning to vice was not an option, because it never left.

In August following the raids, ASHA released a statement lauding the actions that had been taken and praising Wilson for preserving the honor and integrity of Texas. Less than two months later, it received word that eight houses had been reopened on Market Street, just two blocks north of their previous location on Postoffice Street. It conveniently decided not to immediately confirm these reports with a new survey, perhaps in hopes

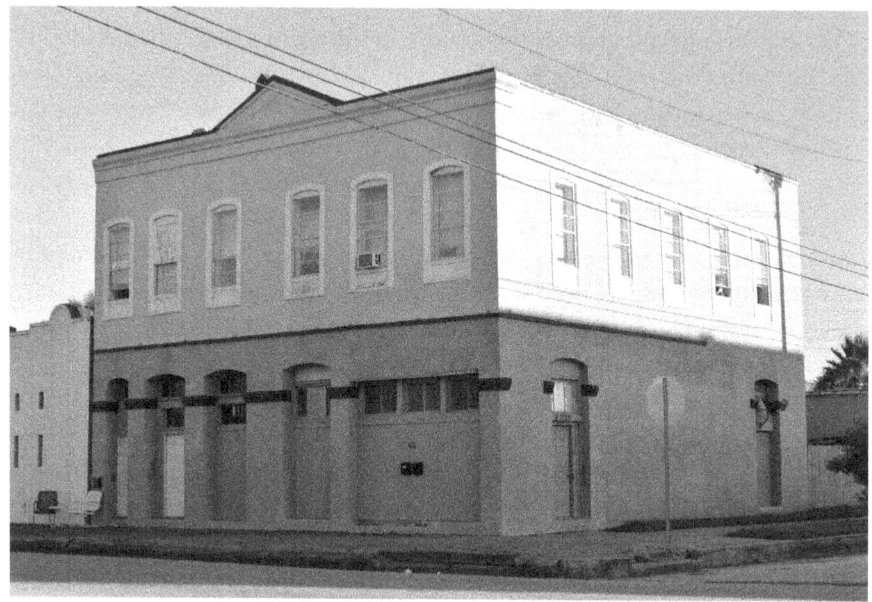

This building at 2727 Market Street operated as a brothel after the Line was shut down in 1953. *Photo by author.*

that postponing would produce more desirable results. Quite the opposite happened, however, and their undercover report in March 1958 revealed that prostitution had risen back up to 50 percent of its former volume and that gambling had actually increased from its levels before the raid.[37]

Several other reports were conducted, but they were relatively ignored, and locals clearly remember that prostitutes were still scattered all over town in the late 1950s.[38] The ASHA remained diligent and committed to its cause, to the point that it was faced with a revealing quandary when Will Wilson's term was up for reelection in 1960. An undercover survey that year revealed not only that prostitution was still rampant but also that gambling was still happening on a large scale even though it had been moved off the seawall and into the business district and was only available to locals. Considering that during the Crime Commission investigation the Maceos were chastised for fleecing Galveston residents when in actuality the majority of their income came from out-of-towners, this was an ironic development for the crusaders.

At the same time, voters of Galveston were poised to decide whether or not to change the city charter and do away with the commission form of government in favor of a mayor-council format. Supporters of the change widely believed that the commission was too prone to corruption, since each of the members oversaw an entire facet of city operations with no accountability. The ASHA believed that Galveston's approval of the new charter would be good for Wilson as a tangible indication of his success, and its survey could actually help to sway islanders to amend the city government, since most of them were assumed to be completely unaware of the level of vice that still remained. On the other hand, the association feared that exposing Wilson's operation as completely ineffective would hurt his chances for reelection.[39]

After much indecision, the association decided at last to release the reports. The news received little national coverage, and the sole concern of the local press was the fact that Galveston had been the only city whose results had been publicized when Houston and San Antonio were also surveyed.[40] No connection at all was made between Wilson's vigilante reclamation of the city and its now revealed shortcomings, and the dissemination of the 1960 survey received nowhere near the attention of the shutdown itself. Unsurprisingly, Wilson served another term as Texas attorney general.

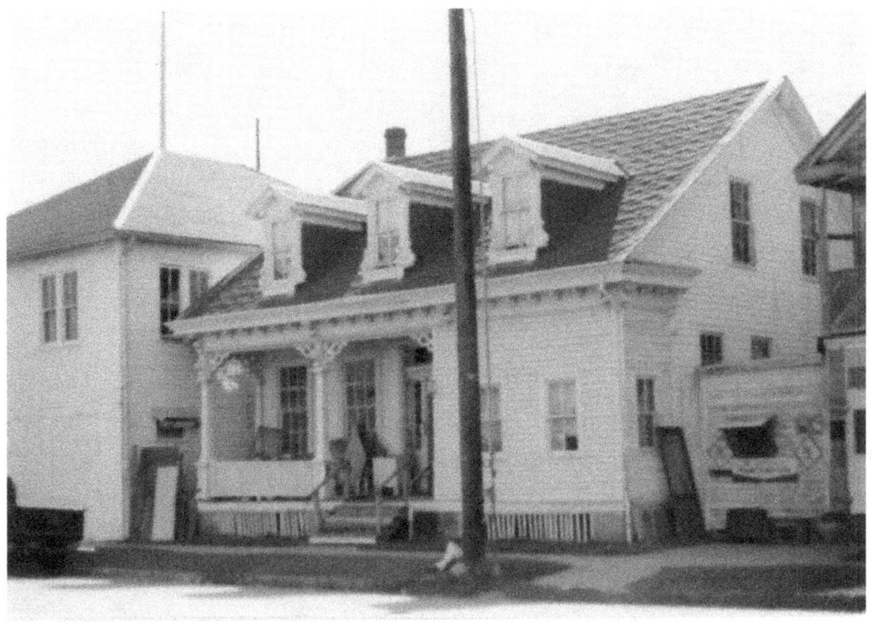

A former brothel located at 2705 Postoffice Street, circa 1965. *Courtesy of Rosenberg Library.*

The final undercover survey of prostitution conditions in Galveston was performed by the ASHA in 1967. Although no traditional brothels remained, it investigated several bars with questionable practices and even the bellhops of the higher-end hotels. In total, it found fewer than fifty working women where at one time there had been more than one thousand.[41] The conductors of the survey more than likely attributed these numbers to the events of the late 1950s, but much had changed in the ensuing decade, not the least of which was an exponential increase in opportunities for women.

As for Galveston, its public decimation at the hands of Will Wilson stunted the city's growth, although possibly not more than a continuance of vice would have. Somewhat jaded and weary, Galvestonians soon found other ways to occupy their time. In the 1960s, the grand but slowly dilapidating downtown buildings from Galveston's nineteenth-century commercial prosperity had now reached the age where they were considered not just old but historic. Local citizens formed groups to prevent them from being demolished and focused their energy on restoring them to their former glory. Along the seawall, 1960s developments such as Sea-Arama Marine World and the Flagship Hotel, the only hotel over the water, helped to establish Galveston as a family-friendly destination, just as Wilson had envisioned.

Part II

The Houses

4

HOOK, LINE AND SINNERS

They were built as symbols of prosperity, perhaps as a weekend home in the most fashionable city in Texas, at a time before internal strife ripped apart a nation and fractured downtown Galveston in the process. Prior to this, the wharf and the city's business district had been established on the eastern end of the island. It was bordered to the north by the harbor and the wharf, the physical muscles of the city's figurative port economy; to the east and west by Nineteenth and Twenty-Fifth Streets, respectively; and to the south by Market Street, one block away from Postoffice Street. Galveston's earliest residential areas naturally grew up around all three sides of the district.

When Union troops occupying the island decided that the commercial area needed to expand, they pushed it south toward Broadway Avenue, effectively creating an insurmountable crevasse between the surrounding residences. Somehow, the area to the east of the divide was decided upon as the choice residential zone, while the area to the west seemed more suitable for industry. As this western area began to rapidly decline in aesthetic value and houses were often demolished to make way for commercial structures, the few blocks of houses that remained on Postoffice west of Twenty-Fifth Street seemed to be preparing for a different destiny and suddenly became almost worthless.[1] But all it took was one business-savvy madam to notice that these beautiful and massive structures with several bedrooms were not only cheap but also in the perfect location for their business—located close enough to the seaport full of businessmen and ship crews to be convenient, but far enough away to be considered a respectable distance.

Needless to say, very little changed on the Line in the way of architecture over the course of its seventy-year existence, even though most of the original houses predated that by another thirty years. The only new construction on this section of Postoffice documented after this time was in 1886.[2] The houses certainly got older and uglier and fell further and further into disrepair, but the ambiance they exuded, the stories they told and the secrets they kept is a vision that has never aged.

On any given summer day, at any given time in the early twentieth century, Postoffice Street bakes under the shameless heat of a Texas sun. Although the sun does nothing to burn through the stifling air saturated with humidity, it unabashedly illuminates every fleck of peeling white paint along the block and the curious way the porches are all surreptitiously hidden by latticework and only the top halves of the windows have shutters. Each house seems quieter than the next, as if every person inside is for some reason asleep in the middle of the day. The only interruption of the silence is the occasional roar of a delivery truck passing through or the ding of the streetcar that does not stop, either. Sometimes, though not often, the familiar sound of a screen door slamming against the back of a house will echo through the alleyway, followed by a sleek and shiny new sedan pulling out onto the street.[3]

Elsewhere in the city, the respectable folk of Galveston go about their business—unloading freight at the docks, making deals on the Strand, taking walks underneath the shade of a parasol and the enormous trees that line Broadway's grand esplanade. As the shadows stretch out toward the east and the sun begins its daily trek to the other side of the world, "Closed" signs are placed in shop windows and parents and their children stream into dining rooms for family dinner. Then, slowly, one by one, the lights in the windows dim, father retires to his study while mother dismisses the servants and tucks the children into bed. And at that precise moment, the houses of Postoffice Street come alive.

Windows are thrown open, and the space unfettered by shutters is at once filled with a backlit Romanesque tableau of a beautiful woman, with just enough of her covered to keep the mystery alive. As cars start to pile in, slowly careening down each block and back again, the goddess image of the woman in the window is shattered as she calls out lewdly to a young sailor and the sleeve of her shorty pajamas dips seductively off of her shoulder. The man calls back but decides to shop around before making his choice.

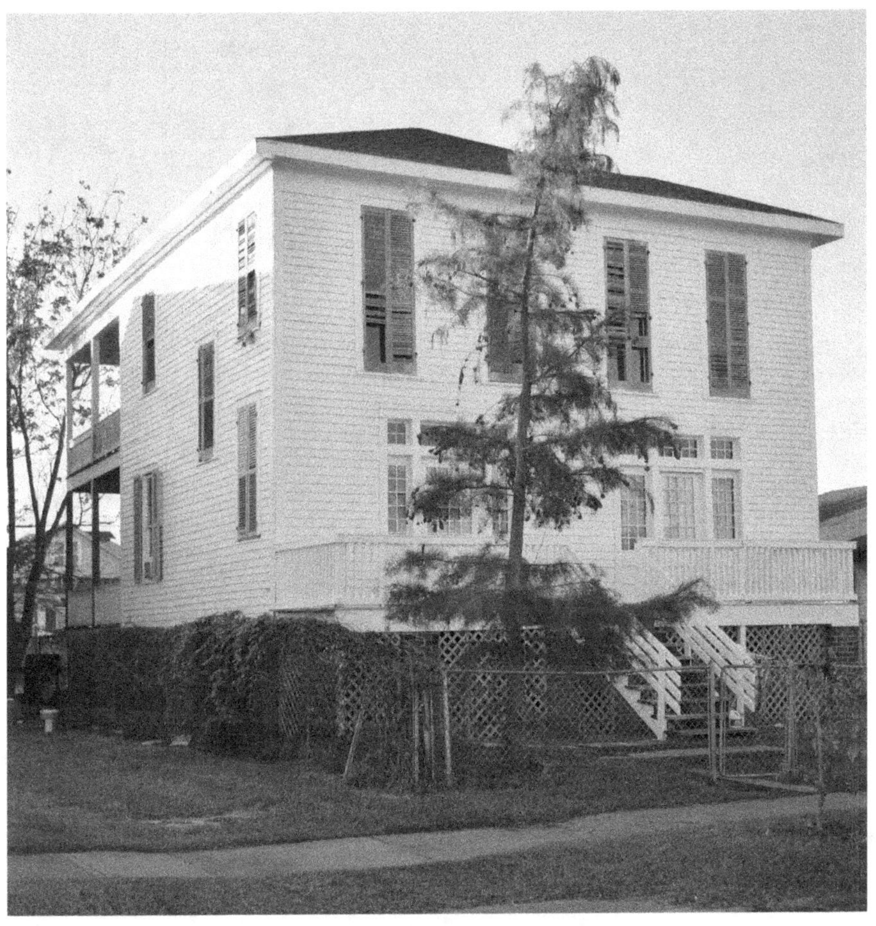

Currently a residence, the house at 3311 Ball Street was built as a brothel in the district's later years. *Photo by author.*

House after house, down the Line he goes, the same images taunting him, beckoning him to come inside.

The location of the houses in the district was no secret; even the young students over at the primary school knew where they were and how to recognize them.[4] Just like mimetic architecture that advertises what is inside, they were easy to spot with their uniform white paint and shutters painted green or battleship gray.[5] But the madams who ran the houses did not rely on word of mouth and knew how to get their hooks in to new clients and outsiders unfamiliar with the terrain. Without the convenience of the Internet or a computer that fits in their pocket, these enterprising women

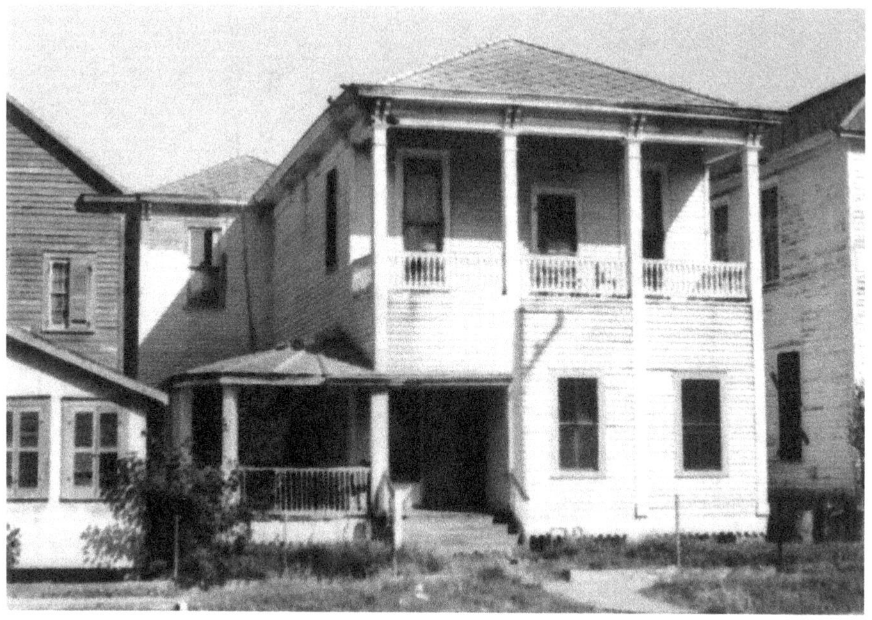

A former bordello located at 2710 Postoffice, circa 1966. *Courtesy of Rosenberg Library.*

used every trick in the book to ensure that the presence and location of their houses were widely known and readily available to the right people.

The most basic form of advertising was the listing of the houses in the annual city directories that were published in Galveston. Each directory included the typical alphabetical listings of residences and businesses, but it also included a section organized numerically by street addresses in which one could simply pick out a certain block of the city, say, Postoffice Street between Twenty-Fifth and Twenty-Ninth Streets, and peruse its contents. Each address listing in this section was accompanied by the name of the homeowner for residential addresses and the name of the business for commercial addresses. The well-known madams usually owned their own houses and simply used their own names, but madams who were not so high profile or who rented their establishments realized that it was much more beneficial to give their houses a business name that was obvious but not too obvious to a curious someone who was scrolling through the Postoffice Street section. This resulted in rather unusual additions to the city directory such as the Hilarity Club and the Seventy-Two Club.[6]

However, the houses were not always positioned within the segregated district. At times of peak prostitution in Galveston, their locales spanned

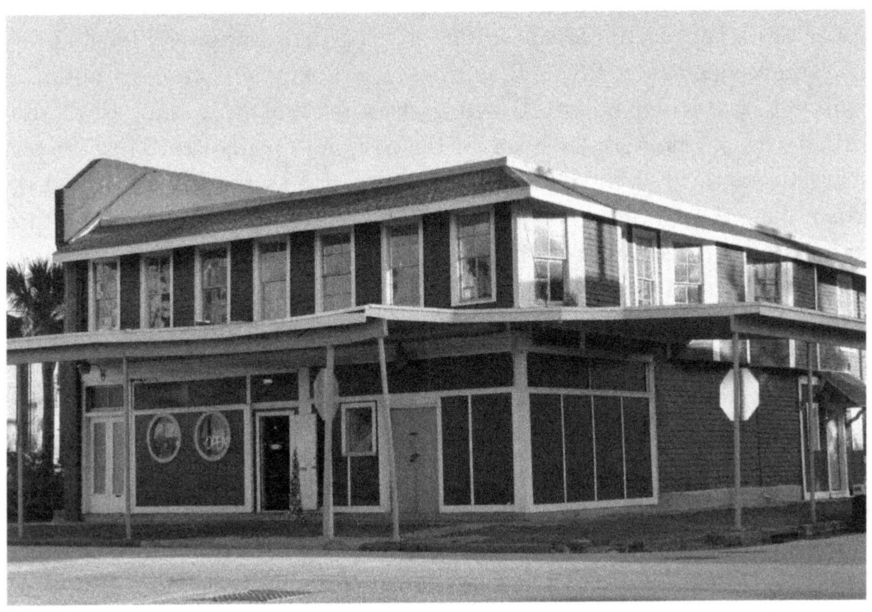

This downtown brothel at the corner of Twenty-Fourth and Church Streets featured a legitimate business downstairs and cribs upstairs. *Photo by author.*

the entirety of the downtown area from Twentieth Street to Thirty-Third Street, and those in more auspicious locations had to do more to blend in with their surroundings. Houses within the actual business district were usually two-story buildings with a large main entrance to a bar or restaurant on the ground floor and an obscure side door that opened onto a set of stairs leading to the second floor, where the brothel rooms were located. These downtown houses with both a main entrance and a side entrance usually had two listings in the city directory and a slight change in name to denote the difference between the two doors, such as a location near the harbor called the Rainbow Club. The popular nightclub was listed at an address of 114 Twentieth Street, but the curious side door with an address of 116 Twentieth Street was called the Rainbow Room.[7]

The location of the red-light district was chosen primarily because of its proximity to seamen and businessmen traveling about the city on foot, but the rise of automobile ownership along with Galveston's notoriety as a gambling destination abruptly made it accessible and sought after by a whole new demographic. The auto industry also inadvertently provided the Line with services from local taxicab drivers, who found a way to profit off of the district and make extra income. Inevitably, the drivers discovered that a workday rarely passed without one of their customers looking for an extracurricular activity, and so they would arrange symbiotic business deals with particular houses. It was a steep investment on the part of the girls, however, who bore the brunt of the cost, not the madam. Most drivers charged one-third of the house's going rate for the service being provided, which the girl paid on top of her required fee to the madam, and thus this resource was the least desirable of all those available. Especially on busy nights when much more lucrative clients were readily at hand, often the men who arrived by taxi would find themselves rather coolly received.[8]

During times when the district was closed, women often had to resort to direct solicitation on the streets and in bars, but otherwise these instances were rare. The ladies of the Line were known to use the telephone to drum up business on days when traffic was slow. Every house had a coin-operated pay phone, and at times the girl would invest a nickel to place a call to Fort Crockett, the twenty-four-hour diners and, sometimes, their regular customers. They would even ring the newspaper offices when the late-night shifts were working in the mechanical and editing rooms, pretend to query the outcome of a sports game or some other triviality and then steer the conversation in the direction of their house.[9]

In the 1930s, an opposite trend emerged in the form of the call girl system. It was typically seen only at the high-end brothels, where the girls could afford to have calling cards printed and were allowed by their madam to venture east of Twenty-Fifth Street, where they would pass them out while mingling in respectable places. The calling cards were also offered to the girls' better customers in the hopes that they would return; this would also allow them to schedule clients during the hours when the brothel was closed in order to maximize their daily profit.

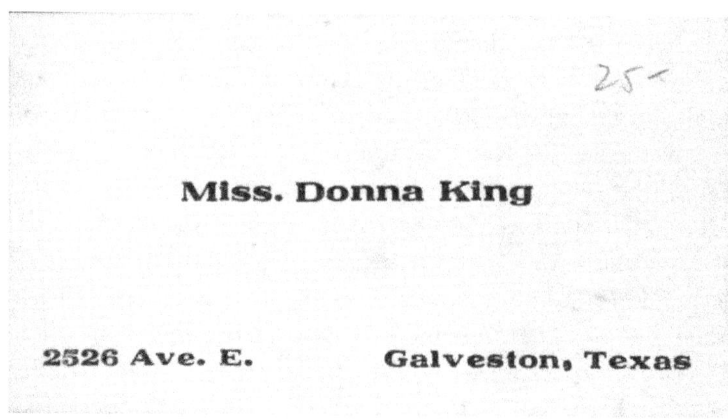
25¢

Miss. Donna King

2526 Ave. E. **Galveston, Texas**

Calling card for a girl named Donna King. *Courtesy of Rosenberg Library.*

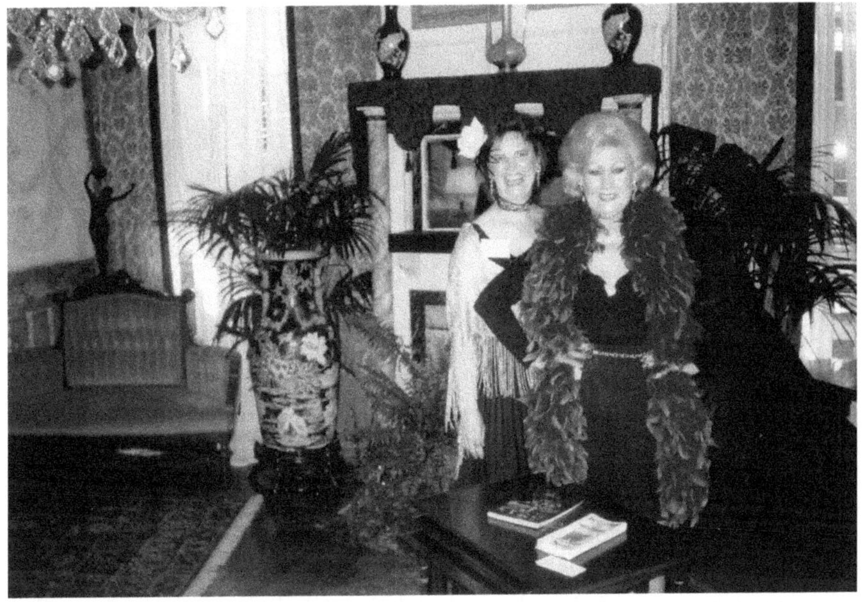

A view of the interior parlor of Mother Harvey's, taken in 1992 during the Annual Homes Tour hosted by Galveston Historical Foundation. *Photo provided anonymously.*

Standard hours for houses on the Line were 6:00 p.m. to 2:00 a.m., seven days a week.[10] Once the house had opened for the evening, business operations inside were kept relatively efficient and streamlined. Men would knock at the door and wait to be inspected by the housemaid through the peephole, all the while cleverly concealed by the strategically placed lattice. Upon entering the house, he was graciously welcomed by the madam, who would escort him to the parlor or sitting room, the appearance of which highly depended on the house. The more expensive houses featured lush furniture, often of the Victorian style in which the house was built, but one was said to have no more than wooden benches. Each sitting area, no matter its furnishings, almost always included a bar that served only wine, whiskey and beer, as well as a coin-operated music box on the wall and bare wooden floors for dancing.[11] The first floor also included a small room for the maid and the madam's quarters, which in smaller houses would sometimes double as the parlor, but more often than not it was entirely off-limits without a personal invitation.

The men would be encouraged to buy drinks for themselves and for the girls, to keep the music box churning with their quarters and to dance a number or two. After this, they would be led upstairs. The second floor of the house was divided into a number of small rooms, each featuring little more than a bed, a washbasin and a lock on the door. Construction of that period utilized transoms above each interior door to help with air flow, but some madams used them as a security measure and required them to be left open so they could hear what was going on inside each room.[12] And that usually depended on how much the john had to spend. The stock service was a "straight quickie" for fifteen minutes, and houses also had established rates for "French" services, a slang term for oral sex; or half and half, half regular and half French. Full hours were available as well, usually for a slight discount, but whole nights were pay-to-play and were not sold at a bargain.[13]

Inner house accounting systems were clever but rigid, with no room for error or moonlighting, although gifts were more than acceptable and not counted toward a girl's "take." At the downtown bordellos with the side doors, the caller would have to pay and get a paper ticket at the foot of the stairs before venturing up to a large dance floor and bar area that was directly adjacent to a long hallway. This hallway led to a row of small cribs, at the end of which was a washbasin situated next to another set of stairs leading down to an exit into the alleyway.[14]

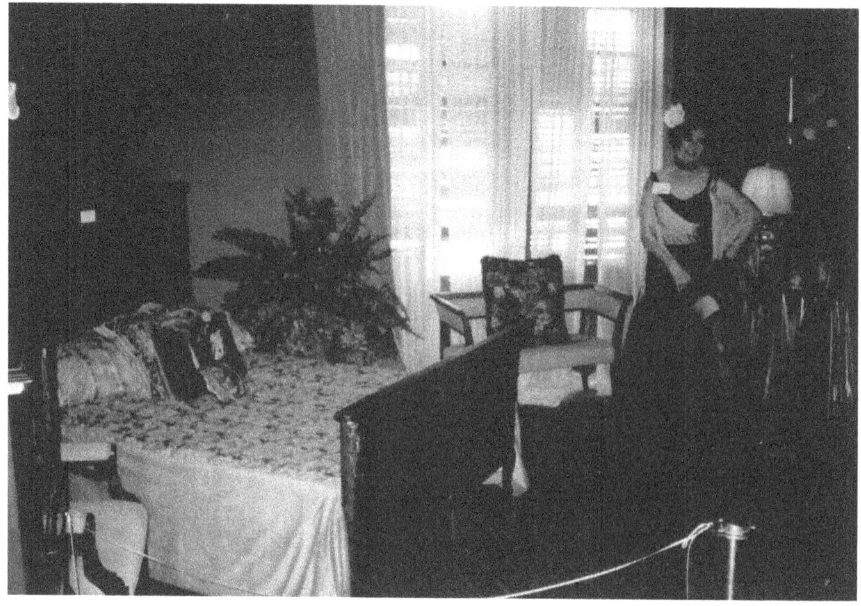

An upstairs bedroom of Mother Harvey's bordello, taken during the Homes Tour. *Photo provided anonymously.*

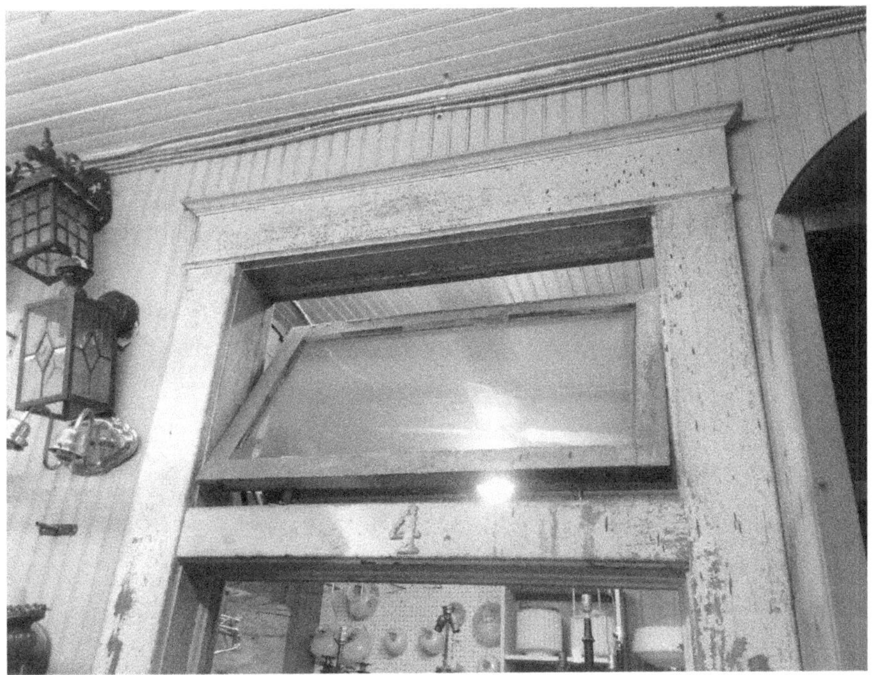

Transoms above the bedroom doors, like this one in the former Oleander Hotel, were used by the madam to keep watch on her girls. *Photo by author.*

At district houses where various entrances and exits were open all over the house to allow for discretion, they had much more room for error and so the maid would often sit at a desk at the foot of the stairs and employ whatever system the madam had in place. One simple but clever system used towels to keep track of a girl's customers. As she walked up the stairs, the maid would hand her a towel and record the time. After she collected the money, it would be sent down to the maid in a little box attached to a string, or sometimes it would simply be thrown to her from upstairs. At the end of the night, the number of towels in a girl's possession had to match the maid's ledger.[15]

In the 1940s, at the district's peak, it has been estimated that one house could bring in $15,000 to $20,000 a week.[16] Such an exorbitant sum, however, was often drastically reduced by raids and their ensuing fines, doctor bills, health certificates and, most excessive, the cost of doing business in Galveston.

5
THE SPACE BETWEEN

Collectively among the bawdy houses of Galveston was a very distinct hierarchy, most obvious to the consumer in the prices but also reflected in the level of service outside the bedrooms. High-end or premier houses presented their girls in flowing evening gowns, and the women did not appear in the parlor until their scheduled appointment arrived or they were summoned by the madam, at which time several girls would be formally presented from whom the gentleman made his choice. Girls at less expensive brothels would wear only shorty pajamas and would often be gathered in the parlor to swoop in and dote on every man who walked in the door.[1]

The prices charged at the houses were certainly indicative of these distinctions, as well as the ages of the girls working—older women were often forced to work for less.[2] On average, during the first half of the twentieth century, houses bottomed out at $1 for fifteen minutes at the seediest locations and during the times when competition was steep. Most commonly, a midlevel brothel would charge $3 but $5 for sailors, presumably because of their high-maintenance nature, potential for rowdiness or propensity for disease.[3] At the premier houses, the same quarter hour would run between $10 and $25, with a staggering price of $300 for the entire evening.[4]

The range of clients who patronized the houses was just as diverse as their offerings. The bulk of steady contributions to the Line were made by longshoremen and sailors from the port, soldiers from Fort Crockett and Fort San Jacinto and young men who were students at the local teaching

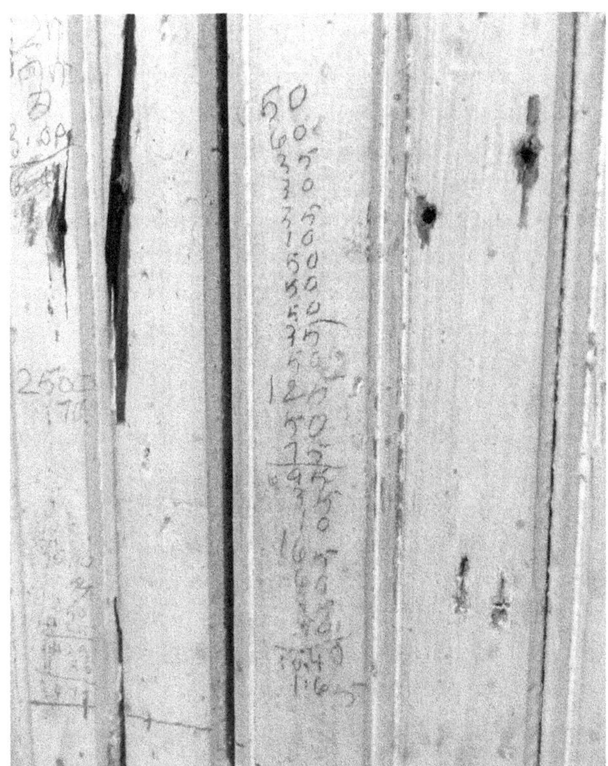

A prostitute kept track of her earnings by scratching them on the wall in the old Oleander Hotel (currently Antique Warehouse). *Photo by author.*

hospital.[5] Local clients included men from all walks of life, from members of the Coast Guard to off-duty police officers, from waiters and shopkeepers to bootleggers and rumrunners.[6] Less reliable were the attendees of conventions and visiting gamblers, but their peak-season volume more than made up for their inconsistency.

Visitors of the esteemed variety were not in shortage, either. President Lyndon B. Johnson and Texas governor Shivers were said to have come to the district to "get lost for a while." Local playboys, most of whom were the scions of elite Galveston families, were known to take over houses on the Line and throw outrageous parties.[7] Some of these parties were gratis, hosted by the madam for good measure. Her guest lists included an eclectic assortment of characters to whom she was the penultimate hostess—attentive and generous with both her liquor and her girls.[8] On other occasions, wealthy clients would buy out a house for an entire night. The doors would be locked, and no one was allowed in or out under any circumstances, much to the delight of a young errand boy who got trapped one evening and was served ice cream and soda until sunrise, when he was finally allowed to leave.[9] Sometimes the parties would last for two or three days. Food was brought in for the guests, and the madam would keep a running tally of drinks and frolicking as the party went on, to be paid in full by the host as his bleary-eyed guests slipped out the back door.[10]

Aside from price, another way some houses set themselves apart was through the use of themes and gimmicks. This technique became most popular later in the 1940s and into the '50s, when competition amped up, but one of the first and most notorious to do it was a madam from the 1920s simply known as Janet. Its regular and robust clientele nicknamed it the "French House," because it specialized in "alternative" sexual methods and, of course, charged higher prices.[11] In the '30s, a brothel known as the Pennsylvania Hotel specialized in corpulent women and flagrantly advertised their "love by the ton."[12]

Other distinct specialty houses included the Spanish House on Twenty-Seventh Street, fully stocked with gorgeous women from all over Central and South America, and the Cajun House, which featured tall, slim Louisiana girls with dark skin and thick accents whom all the men considered "foreign" and exotic.[13] Houses that specialized in male homosexual prostitution were few in number and always located away

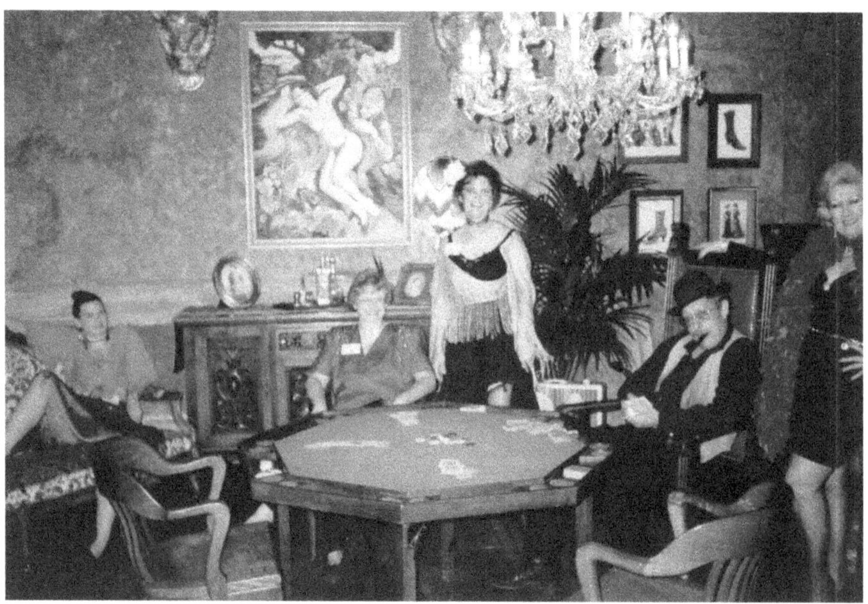

The large parlor of Mother Harvey's, where she would entertain guests, was another feature of the Homes Tour. *Photo provided anonymously.*

from the red-light district, in small hotels along the beachfront and next to Union Station at Twenty-Fifth and Strand, as well as on one particularly shady street with ample coverage from a group of resplendent palm trees.[14] But the one house that caused more head turns than all of the others combined was one run by a black woman who was coupled with a white man; not surprisingly, her house supplied the same combination, which was highly frowned upon in the Jim Crow era.[15] In fact, her existence may be nothing but legend, considering that more reliable documentation exists of white women being chased out of town on several occasions for offering their services to black men.[16] Even though this wide spectrum of diversity among Galveston prostitutes was a direct reflection of the same diversity present in the island population, the standard practices of the era still applied to all people not of Caucasian background, prostitute or not.

Ranking among the houses in the district was also a direct product of the stark and uncompromising racial divides that existed at the time. Houses that employed nonwhite women could not be located directly on Postoffice Street but instead took up in smaller shanties along the adjacent alleyways as well as on Church Street to the south, Mechanic Street to the north and most of the intersecting numbered streets.[17] These areas were by far the least expensive of the district and were often branded with colorful nicknames, such as Tincan Alley, Superstitious Alley,[18] Bleiches Alley and the Plantation.[19] Quite a few of them, such as Margaret's Tea Room at 711 Twenty-Ninth Street and the Mississippi House at 2713 Church Street, catered especially to white men who could not afford the higher prices or who were in search of variety. Black men, however, were never allowed inside the brothels on Postoffice.[20]

The atmosphere within these outlying houses was far rowdier than even the wildest establishments of Postoffice Street, partly because they were the only houses that allowed gambling in the form of craps, which could often get out of hand. These bordellos were also bigger targets for the police, considering that they were in fact legally recognized when the city passed anti-miscegenation laws, the only law regarding prostitution that local police officers actually enforced. On other occasions, the black houses would simply be the victims of an innately low level of respect for their employees. Caucasian men were known to raise "any kind of hell" they desired in black brothels with no ramifications, because if the slightest resistance was met, all that had to be done was to notify the local beat cop, and he would happily come in and beat the housemates and their similar-skinned patrons senseless.[21]

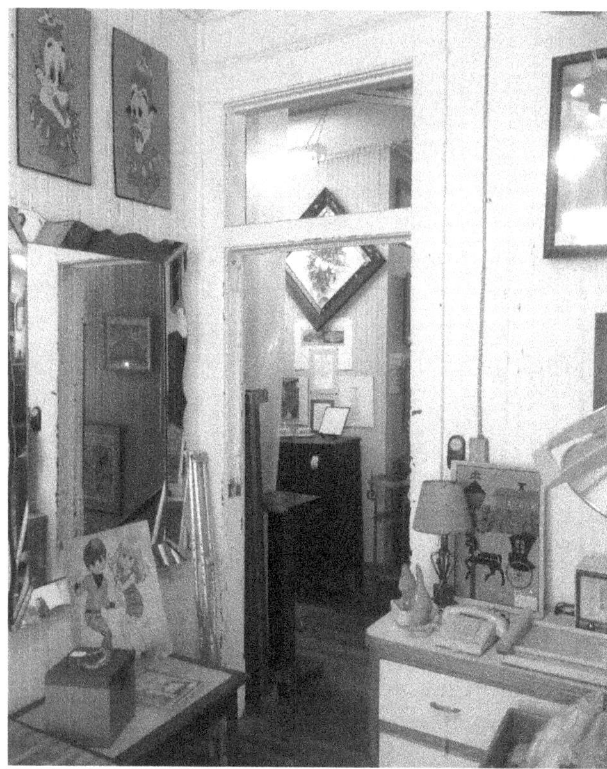

The view from inside one of the twenty-eight cribs on the second floor of the Oleander Hotel. *Photo by author.*

Fortunately, most of the interactions between law enforcement and the women and patrons of the Line were much more civilized. In fact, a typical "raid" usually consisted of the sheriff or police chief placing a phone call to the house to tell the madam that she had been raided. Girls would pile into a vehicle and drive over to the station, where they would pay their fines and leave. The charge was usually misdemeanor-level vagrancy, and the fines averaged $25 per girl, although the madams could sometimes be charged as much as $225. The next day, the "results" of the raid and the names of those arrested would be printed, and that seemed to satisfy the public and the city coffers to an immense degree, something the Line accomplished in more ways than one.[22]

6

REMNANTS OF RED LIGHTS

At its peak, the red-light district is best estimated to have contained fifty-four houses of prostitution[1] and an average over its lifespan of fifty houses at a time.[2] Those numbers do not include the various cribs and hotel rooms scattered about the city, nor the houses along the beach, throughout downtown or out on the west end, where premier establishments chose to build in later years. If the estimates of the brothels' weekly intake are correct, one house could alone could pull in as much as $1 million in one year. Leaving out the operations outside the district, and even if that yearly estimate is only correct by half, prostitution was a $25 million per year industry in Galveston, roughly eight times the annual gross income of the Maceos.[3] The dynamic economic influence of numbers such as these is unquestionable, especially on a city with a population of roughly fifty to sixty thousand, depending on the decade. The positive impact of red-light houses was apparent at the time, and enough of it still lingers today to offer a candid view into this clandestine world.

In the late 1940s, the Galveston district had swelled again to the level of influence it maintained between the two world wars, and the benefits were reaped not only by the madams and the girls. Prostitution employed more than eight hundred people in the form of girls, madams, maids, pimps and taxi drivers.[4] Furthermore, the girls rarely traveled and loved to spend their cash, which meant that almost the entirety of their income was put back into the city. The expensive downtown department stores full of high-end clothing, such as Nathan's, were there almost exclusively at the behest of

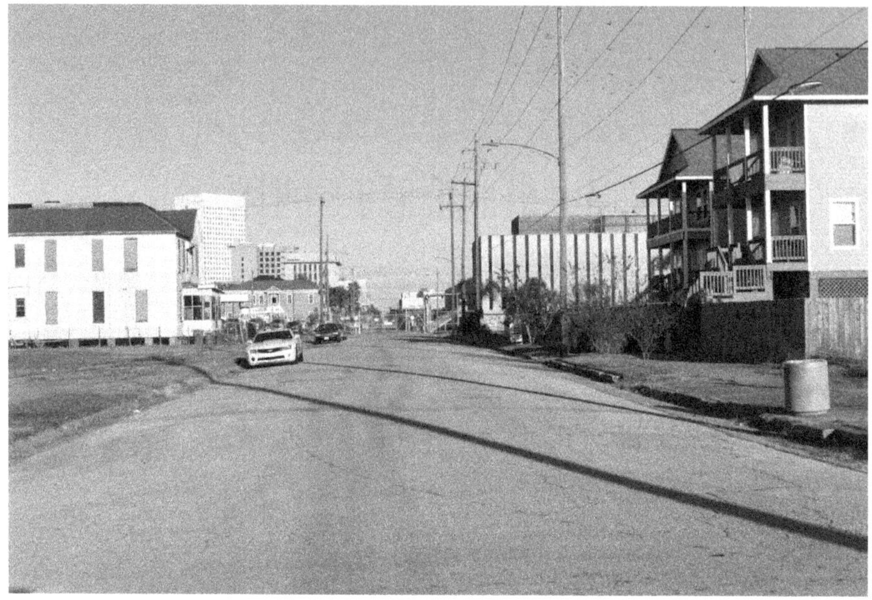

Present-day view of Postoffice Street looking east from Twenty-Eighth Street. The surviving house on the left was not used as a brothel but closely resembles the houses that were; pictured to its right is Mother Harvey's, located one block to the east, with the city power station that occupies the Twenty-Sixth Street block visible in between. *Photo by author.*

the ladies of the Line, and the best customers of the local Cadillac dealer were the pimps and the madams.[5] Waiters, bartenders, hairdressers, shoe salesmen—the far-reaching list of people positively impacted by the houses was endless.

Later, after the curtain had been drawn on Galveston vice, the number of houses dropped to fewer than twenty by 1960 and plummeted further by the end of the decade. The impact of their presence also changed dramatically, from a major economic player, the industry was now only a source of curiosity when its business was still conducted out in the open as it had been during the district days. A restaurant called the Rio Grande on Market Street was located in a building that had been used as a brothel since the late 1950s, when the girls and madams were forced off the Line. A decade later, people would be regularly seen going up and down a very prominently placed staircase, back and forth from the cribs upstairs, right in the middle of someone's dinner or spin around the dance floor.[6]

The very last known house of prostitution in Galveston actually survived until the early 1990s, cleverly disguised as a small hotel. Just across from

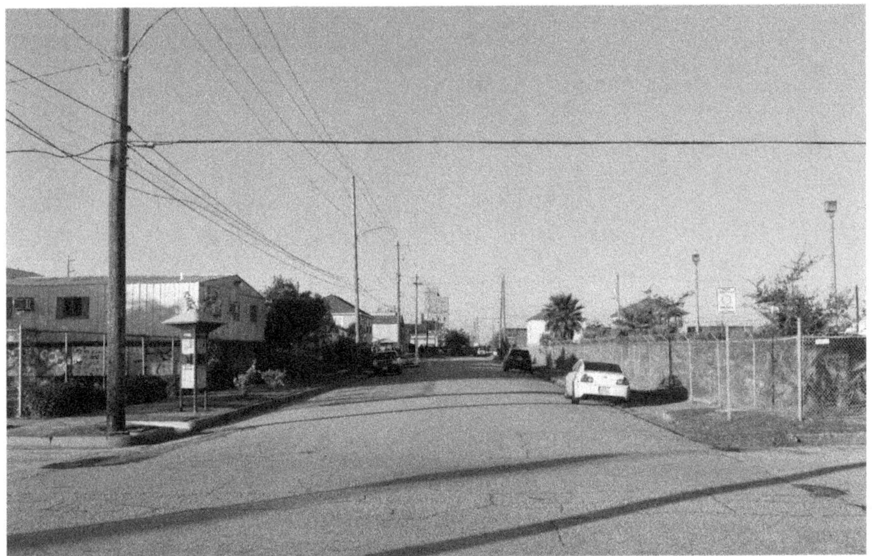

Present-day view of Postoffice Street looking west from Twenty-Eighth Street. *Photo by author.*

the old Union Station at Twenty-Fifth and Strand, a curious block-shaped building encompasses the entire length of Twenty-Sixth Street between Santa Fe Place and Mechanic Street. During its heyday in the 1950s, the building featured an attached garage on the back side of the building so that men could pull their cars in and walk inside without being seen. In the 1980s, a gambling house was situated right next door, which made for a rather busy intersection at all hours of the night. The building's interior was later renovated into two nightclub spaces and the garage converted into a patio. Currently, it is home to Havana Alley Cigar Shop & Lounge.[7]

One of the most intact relics of Galveston's red-light days is now an antiques salvage shop called the Antique Warehouse, located on the northwest corner of Twenty-Fifth Street and Postoffice. It was once a segregated rooming house called the Oleander Hotel, later converted into a bordello. The layout of the second floor remains untouched; twenty-eight small rooms circle the inner and outer perimeters of the second floor, with an atrium in the center of the interior rooms and one long continuous hallway connecting it all. One larger room on the outside wall doubled as the madam's room and the parlor, where the girls would line up for the customers. The smallest room, located along one of the interior rows, was the only bathroom for thirty women.[8]

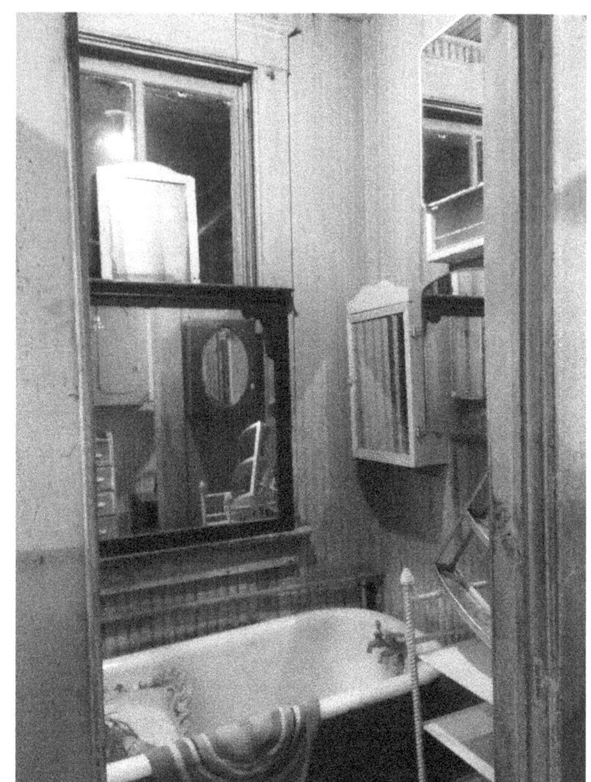

Right: Upstairs at the Oleander Hotel, twenty-eight girls shared this one small bathroom. *Photo by the author.*

Below: The building that currently houses Havana Alley was an operating brothel disguised as a hotel until the early 1990s. *Photo by author.*

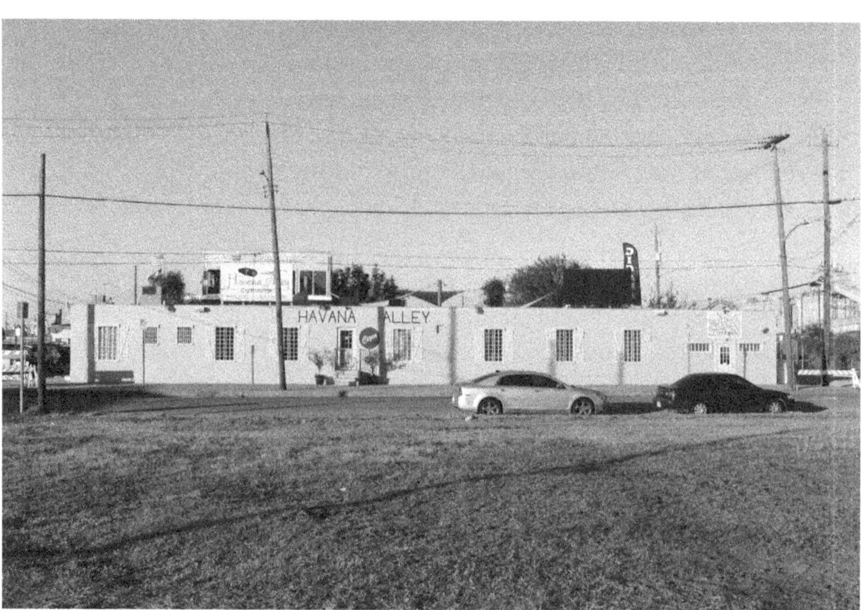

Another symbol of the red-light district that lingers downtown is the subtle and mysterious side door. Unlike the houses on Postoffice that were converted from single-family domiciles, a handful of houses that were built within the downtown commercial district were actually designed to be brothels. Since houses in the business district actually had to look like businesses, the bottom floors were constructed to house some combination of restaurants, bars and nightclubs. The brothel was upstairs, but in order to eliminate suspicion for their legitimate customers—men constantly walking up and down the stairs in plain sight—a separate, smaller entrance was added to the exterior that led only to a staircase. A locally owned bar called the Wizz is presently located inside one of these rare remaining buildings, located on the southeast corner of Twenty-Fourth and Church Streets, and a small market called Fiesta inhabits another, the former Rainbow Room on Twentieth Street half a block south of Harborside Drive.

Over on Market Street between Twenty-Seventh and Twenty-Eighth Streets is where the Line's occupants sought refuge after their eviction in 1957, and several buildings remain that were used as bordellos at least until the late 1960s.[9] Incidentally, they are located directly across the street from the Maceo Spice & Import Company; although the Maceos were not at all directly involved in prostitution, they are inextricably linked as the symbols

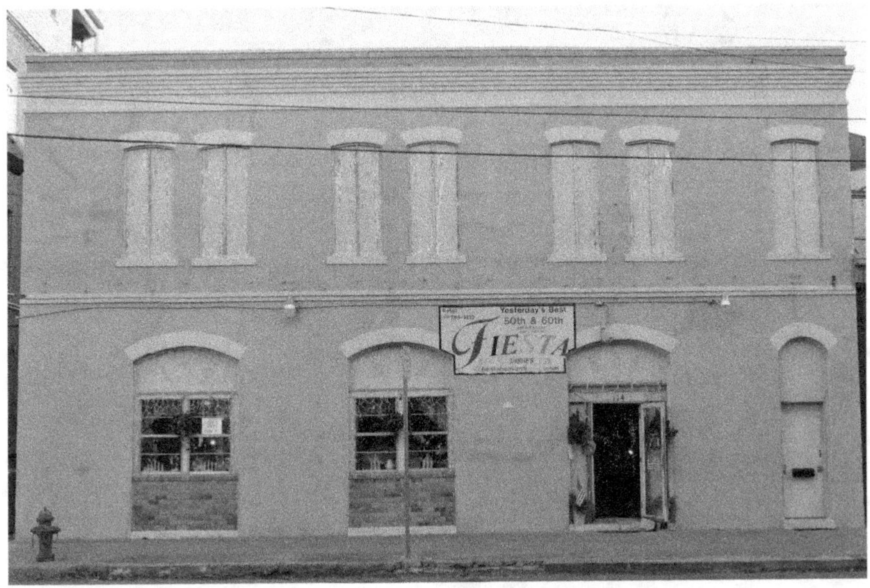

The former Rainbow Club at 114 Twentieth Street had a side door with an address of 116 that led directly to an upstairs bordello called the Rainbow Room. *Photo by author.*

of an era. The Market Street locations now house popular local businesses Daquiri Time Out and Gypsy Joynt.

Houses that remain from the district are few and far between. The famous boardinghouse built by Mollie Waters in 1886 still stands at 2528 Postoffice Street. Now occupied as a residence, it is most well known as Mother Harvey's, where several young men of Galveston, including future mayor Herbert Cartwright, learned to dance under the supervision of the infamous madam. In the 1990s, the house was opened up to the public and placed on the Annual Homes Tour given by the Galveston Historical Foundation. Curious onlookers caught a rare, firsthand glimpse of a house that had long since been accustomed to playing host to strangers. The interior tour featured a downstairs parlor for receiving guests that was typical of brothels at the time, the madam's room, a large anteroom for entertaining and the upstairs cribs used by prostitutes. The only other remaining house from the district to be expressly identified as a brothel is a residence at 3311 Ball Street, and its distance from the Line indicates just how large the district grew to be.

As for the Line itself, the Oleander Hotel remains on the Twenty-Fifth Street corner of Postoffice Street, and at the other end of this same block is Mother Harvey's on the corner of Twenty-Sixth Street. West of that, not a

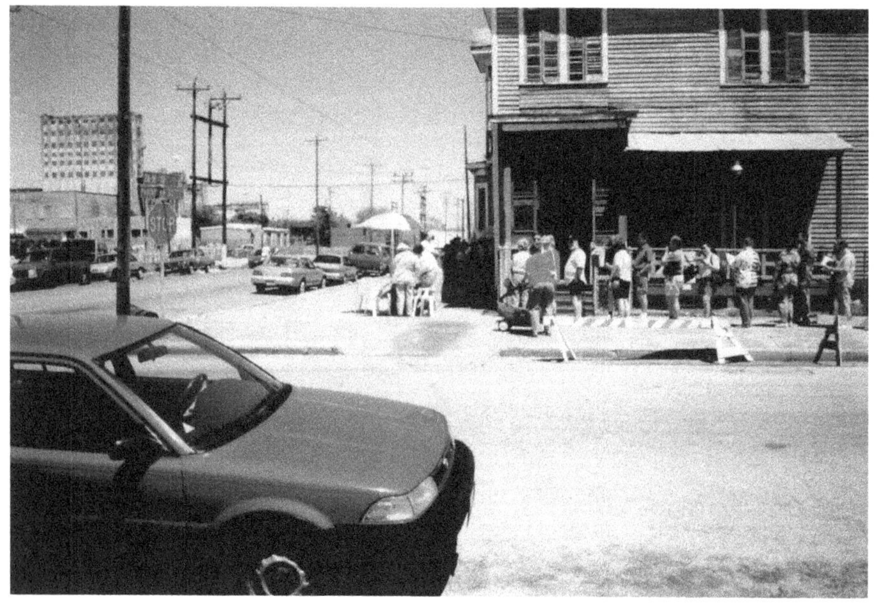

A line forms outside of Mother Harvey's for the 1992 Homes Tour. *Photo provided anonymously.*

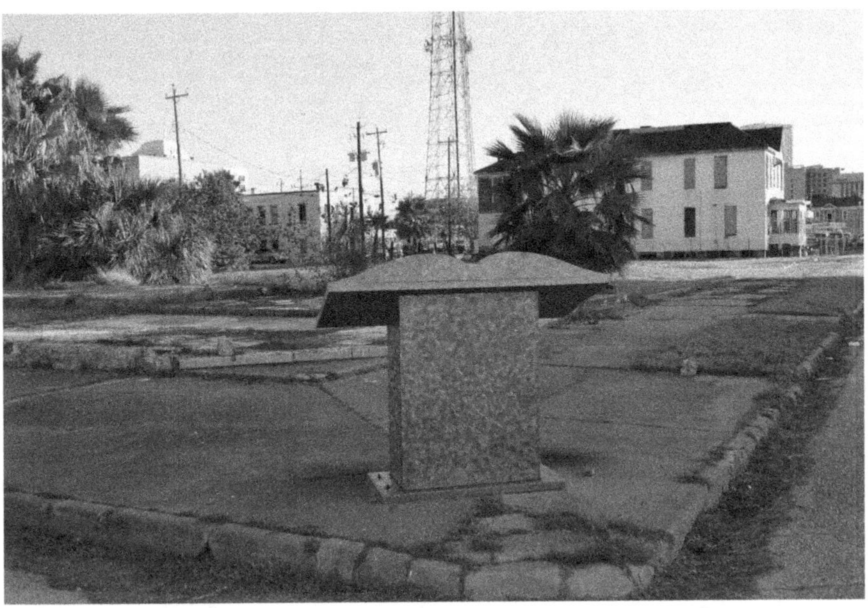

A statue of a Bible sits on the northeast corner of Twenty-Eighth Street and Postoffice. *Photo by author.*

shred of the red-light district remains. The entire Twenty-Sixth Street block is fenced off, taken over by an electric power station. One house on the corner of Twenty-Seventh and Postoffice looks like it was a brothel, right down to its white paint and green shutters, but according to the owner, that particular house was not in fact used as a house of prostitution. The Line did bring in several other businesses to the street, such as barbers, tailors and taverns, and this would be the only explanation as to why it was not demolished when that was the fate of every last house for the next three blocks. Some of the lots are vacant, and others have modern residential construction; a large portion of the rest is dedicated to a nonprofit organization called St. Vincent's Hope Clinic. And perhaps as a declaration that Galveston has seen the error of its ways, or maybe in an attempt to sanctify the sins of the past, the lone occupant of the northeast corner of Twenty-Eighth Street and Postoffice is a large statue of an open Bible.

Part III

The Madams

7

MOTHER MAY I

Civilized society owes much more to madams than it realizes. Tales of how the West was won do not mention that conquering the uncivilized terrain was a losing battle until a few fearless and shrewd women stepped in. Before madams arrived on the scene, most "towns" were merely work camps full of men with nowhere to spend their money. The money that madams made from their conveniently captive audience they invested into general stores, clothing shops, hotels and schools; they even bought entire towns. A spattering of tent cities was now on its way to becoming a network of legitimate municipalities. Madams did not settle Galveston, but they were here at the onset of its founding and have since left a substantial impression in a city already known for its venerable collection of visionary personalities.

Becoming a madam was certainly no one's childhood dream; almost the only path to this profession is through prostitution. Girls who decided to go into business for themselves would often work until their late twenties before venturing out on their own. The average age of madams seemed to get younger as the twentieth century progressed, seemingly because prostitution became a less lucrative profession and more women were choosing to cut ties with the profession sooner.[1] However, this does not take into account that, while girls could often jump from house to house within the same town if conditions were found to be more favorable elsewhere, being a madam could be a very transient life; many of them moved several times in their life to chase the latest hot spot.

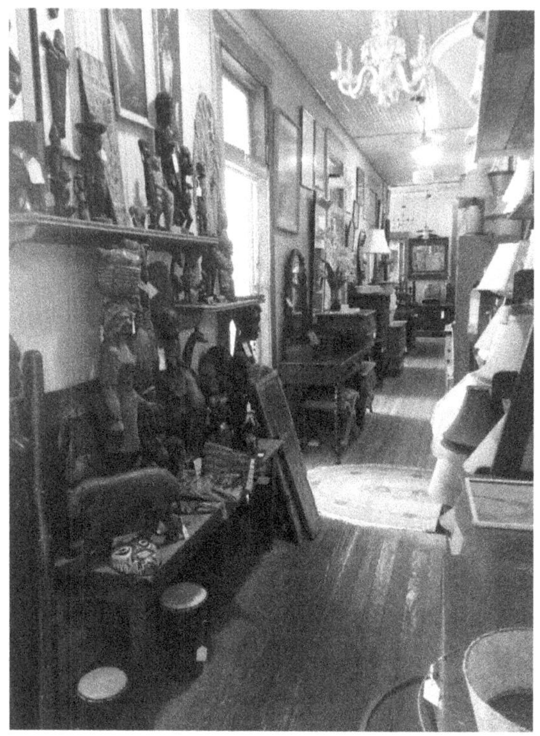

Upstairs at the former Oleander Hotel, one continuous hallway wraps around the entire second floor and connects all twenty-eight rooms. *Photo by author.*

Once at their new location, they would need to discreetly establish themselves as landladies with boardinghouses to one part of the population and then not so discreetly make their true business known to the other. A prostitute's success could be greatly assisted by her beauty, but often that had already been squandered by the ravages of the profession by the time she made it to madam. If a madam was to be as successful in leading a house as she was in working a room, she would need to possess social graces, an aptitude for diplomacy and a keen intellect.[2] These would be required for establishing her integrity with clients and employees, interfacing with politicians whose acceptance of her trade was crucial for her survival and maintaining a sound financial status that could survive raids, sudden lulls in business, possible relocation and, hopefully, retirement.

Each madam ran her respective house with a different yet equally strict set of rules, the severity of which typically depended on whether the operation was luxury or low-end. At the finer houses, the madams allowed and often encouraged the girls to venture out on the town but always made sure they were tastefully dressed and immaculately groomed, to give no immediate evidence of their profession.[3] Often at the less prominent houses, however, a girl could be grounded for up to a year if she was caught east of Twenty-Fifth Street.[4] No matter the house's prosperity, however, madams would not abide dissent between her girls, and "pugnacious temperaments" were not tolerated because of their negative effect on business.[5]

In some instances, girls complained of madams whose accounting skills were lacking, which often resulted in them being overcharged; others recounted feelings of enslavement to a madam who seemed to want to keep their girls in debt and beholden to them.[6] But overall, the majority sentiment was that madams' relationships with their girls were affectionate, protective and motherly. They would have bell systems installed in the houses to warn girls of an impending raid and require either open transoms or unlocked doors to make sure that none of the women were inappropriately treated by a john. Some madams would not force their girls to work if for any reason they were indisposed for an evening. If a pimp was putting pressure on one of the madam's girls, she would call around to other madams to drum up extra work for her.[7]

The leading ladies were equally if not more gracious with their clients, who often turned to the madams for much more than physical gratification. One particular madam had a client who loved poetry, so she memorized his favorite poem to recite for him, as well as a captain who would call her every time he docked. She would pick him and his crew up in her shiny new Cadillac, and they would spend their entire leave at the house, often taking the madam and her girls out for dinner and dancing.[8] Others would host lavish parties for their best clients that began after the brothel closed at two o'clock in the morning and did not end until sunrise. A seaman would often disembark with $2,000 or $3,000 in cash and head straight down to the district to see his madam. She would stash his earnings safely in an envelope for him, let him have his fun for the evening and then return the cash the next morning after deducting whatever he had spent. Sometimes, they would even leave the money with her until they returned on the next leg of their voyage.

These instances of friendship and camaraderie displayed by the madams were a large reason for the Line's collective reputation as a safe, gentlemanly and fair place to do business.[9] Another asset was their adeptness at discretion. Gentlemen were always assured that their anonymity was guaranteed, and keeping that promise was of the utmost importance. The very request for privacy designated a person of esteem and influence whose attention could undoubtedly be directed at certain law enforcement officials. It was simply good business for the madams to be discreet, and the respect was passed

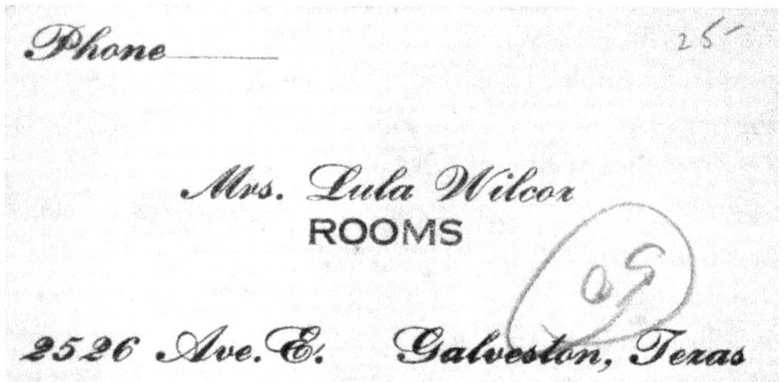

A calling card for a popular madam named Lula Wilcox, whose house was at 2526 Postoffice, next door to Mother Harvey's. *Courtesy of Rosenberg Library.*

The back of Lula Wilcox's calling card dated June 16, 1930. The writing appears to say "one hundred dollars," but the last word is illegible. *Courtesy of Rosenberg Library.*

along even to the average customer. A railway operator stopped at a house in the district one night on his way home from work and passed away while he was there. The madam telephoned the director of a local funeral home, who promptly retrieved the body out the back door. None of the deceased's family members ever learned where it happened.[10]

Because, after all, a madam did not pursue her profession simply for the advantage of interpersonal relationships. Houses of prostitution were extremely lucrative operations, with a base income that included rent paid by her girls for every crib in the house as well as 40 percent off the top of their nightly earnings.[11] A john paid for the room, too, in addition to the services he requested; this could add another one, four or even ten dollars to his final tab.[12] Additional sources of income for the madam were the overpriced alcohol sold to houseguests, the coin-operated pay phone in the hallway and the coin-fed Victrola or piano, which could easily net an extra forty dollars every evening.[13]

Despite the steady cash revenue, the business still required much personal and financial investment. During the business hours, some madams would stay in their apartments or rooms on the first floor and would only emerge to take a drink with a friend or longtime client, but most of them were actively involved in the goings-on of the evening. The madam would greet guests and sometimes dance with them, push the sale of alcohol while also moderating guests to make sure no one got unruly, and keep tabs on all of her girls, a summation of duties that usually did not allow time for her to take clients herself.[14]

The madam's monetary input into her business covered an array of expenses. Some madams owned their houses, while others paid monthly rent; most all employed at least one maid who would answer the door, serve drinks, tidy the rooms between customers and carry change for the phone and music box.[15] When a madam was fined, the amount due was much higher than for the girls, and often she would pay their fines, too.[16] If raids were not an issue for a madam, that meant that one of the ranking law enforcement officials was on the take, like the sheriff who would start at Twenty-Fifth Street and take a stroll once a month, zigzagging from house to house collecting his payoffs.[17]

Certainly not the least of a madam's investments was the one she made in herself. An air of regality and a distinct image were her greatest assets, and those often required the latest fashions, the trendiest hairdos, expensive jewelry and the shiniest, newest Cadillac. The madams were smart with their money, however, and many, such as Queen Laura from the early 1900s, retired from the business with a substantial savings. One madam purchased a hotel for $50,000 and lived out the rest of her life on the revenue from this and other solid investments.[18] Still other tales belie these instances and tell of madams who hit rock bottom and were forced to sell their expensive possessions.

In the end, it was a life that required full immersion in order to achieve success, and this often led to a socially isolated lifestyle. Although a madam's daily activities were filled with the comings and goings of more people than she could count, few among those were people whom she could trust and even fewer upon whom she could rely if her physical or monetary condition deteriorated. Close friendships were rare.[19] Conversely, the madam was obligated to play friendly to the right people, and her task required the fortitude to forge political alliances with the utmost of ease and decorum. Her very survival depended on it.

8

PROPRIETORS AND POLITICIANS

Perchance if the madams would have been permitted to remain sequestered in their houses and only required to attend to the personal business at hand, the career could have been considered a rather luxurious one. But because of the intricacies of her trade—namely that it was illegal—madams were often and not always happily ushered into the spotlight. Clever, observant and always presentable to the public, the madams were well suited for the task and able to bear the pressure of a life that simultaneously required the finesse of a woman and the grit of a politician. Indeed, madams and drama went together like scandal and politics, but big symbols make for big targets.

Most of the scrutiny aimed at the landladies of the red-light district was placed upon them by outside forces, but on certain occasions they brought it on themselves with high-profile and often violent situations. A madam named Mamie Dyer, who ran a house on the Line sometime prior to the 1940s, had in her employ a sweet young girl who immediately aroused the attention of Mamie's husband. Mrs. Dyer had the reputation of being the jealous type, and although it was never proven, there was really no mystery surrounding the girl when she was found strangled underneath the stands of Galveston's beachside racetrack.[1]

Another madam who remains nameless was said to have had a net worth of over $1 million as well as a spectacular crush on a penniless drifter who worked over at the dry dock. She immediately took to seducing him and spared no expense in the process. She bought him clothes, delivered a brand-new Cadillac to him, gifted him an expensive vacation and even gave him cash. Still, it was not enough to turn his affections from another woman, and he was soon found in a cheap beachside hotel, dead.[2]

Other than rather rare and isolated incidents of violence, the most invasive antagonist in the madam's theater of life was the person who wanted a piece of the profits. Endless versions of this person existed, too, and the only thing that frequented her parlor more than a john was a person wanting a handout. Most frequently, it was a city official. During times of lower tolerance, most of the madams had a pay schedule worked out with a protecting officer or even the police chief or commissioner, but the city found itself broke more than once over the course of the district's existence and likened the madams to their own personal piggy banks.[3] Thus, no matter how many payments were made, she always had to be ready for the surprise "raid" to refill the city's thirsty treasury.

Madams were also personally exploited by individuals. A certain police officer requested a personal loan from a madam one year during the Christmas season. Unfortunately, it was a sum that surpassed even what she was able (or willing) to lend. Upon her refusal, he responded, "Well, I guess I'll have to show you how big my badge is." She coolly replied, "You'll have to, because I don't have that kind of money to loan."[4] Other city officials were known to use the madams for their personal gain, the worst of whom was Commissioner of Fire and Police Walter Johnston in the 1950s, but the government was not the only source of coercion faced by the madams.

Not all of the houses on the Line were owned by the madams who operated them. In fact, the majority were rented, which means that every building's owner had a vested interest in prostitution. The only complete assessment of these property holders was made in 1929, but it is most likely reflective of the Postoffice Street investor portfolio during any given decade. Their occupations were revealed to be a real estate agent, the wives of a butcher and a railroad employee, a city fireman and police officer from Galveston departments, a barber, a grocer, a U.S. Customs official and other local business owners, every single one of whom was decidedly dependent upon the madams' success.[5] And because of the precariousness of her situation, she was often required to subtly supplement incomes above and beyond her required rent or else risk unwanted exposure. In an instance that perfectly illustrates this, a certain police officer owned a carpet installation firm as a side business, and his son was a frequent fixture at the brothel. His father would send him to lay down a piece of carpet on the stairs, but the piece of carpet was too short to cover the stairs, so it would inevitably come up and become a hazard for people walking up and down the stairs. The kid would be sent to pull it up, and then sent back over to lay it down again. The same piece of carpet was pulled up and put down repeatedly, and that was how the officer got paid.[6]

Other forms of conflict that occurred often enough to be considered regular were the startling and curious run-ins with the law that had nothing whatsoever to do with the act of prostitution. Many of the court cases would involve a drunken customer who either misplaced his bankroll and accused the madam of stealing it, or was causing a stir down at the house and refused to leave, in which case the madam would not hesitate to pull a weapon nor hesitate to use it. On one occasion, a security guard from the state penitentiary in Huntsville was in Galveston on businesses and decided to visit the district. Once inside the house, he asked the madam, Mattie Sims, for change for a fifty-dollar bill. After claiming that he did not receive his change, he began beating her. Two musicians providing entertainment in the parlor abruptly knocked him unconscious, the police were called and fifty dollars in change was found in the pocket of one of the musicians. The guard filed charges on all three of them, and Mattie attended court wearing a lovely lavender gown. The guard was unable to give a coherent account of the events that transpired during the evening in question, and the charges were dropped.

Drama was also the ultimate result of overseeing a house full of women. The madams often insisted on fostering friendship among the girls, but since they were all veritably in competition with one another every night of the week, quarrels were prone to break out and sometimes turned rather violent. More frequent than inter-house skirmishes were fierce quarrels between girls from two different houses. Hawking from the windows during business hours was sometimes a heated business, and girls would accuse others of "stealing" their business. A girl named Elsie was the target of attacks from the house across the street for several consecutive days, and so she finally decided to walk over to the house and confront her heckler, Maria Guerrero. No one in Maria's house appreciated Elsie's bravery, and she was left bleeding in the street with knife wounds to her face and chest. After she was adequately recovered, Elsie was called to the stand to give her testimony. Maria was arrested and fined ten dollars plus court costs. Their respective madams were quick to put the feud to rest, threatening to expel from Galveston any girl who provoked any further confrontation.

Fortunately, not all of the madams' interactions with law enforcement, politicians and city officials were unpleasant. In truth, most of the people in power were well aware of the positive economic impact of the district, and many of them chose to form alliances with the more prominent madams, who ultimately proved to be a valuable asset in political maneuverings and even campaigns. The two most influential and intriguing pairings of madams and politics were the relationships between Mary Russel and Mayor Herbert Cartwright, and between Ruth Kempner and Big Tit Marie.

Mayor Cartwright had always had an affinity for madams, being that he was practically weaned on the bosom of Mother Harvey during those tender years as a prepubescent teen. Harvey retired in 1930 and sold her establishment to Mary "Gouch-Eye" Russel, who quickly aligned herself with Cartwright and would eventually become the most successful and powerful madam of the district. She was a fierce recruiter with an eye not only for beauty but also for compatibility with the trade, and she appealed greatly to young college students who aligned with her promise of independence and her example of a successful woman of business. These were also the clean-cut, classy type with fresh faces and bright eyes who were working for tuition and adventure, not survival. The result of Russel's business plan was an empire that lasted nearly a quarter of a century and included three red-light houses and a $40,000 yacht for her husband.[7]

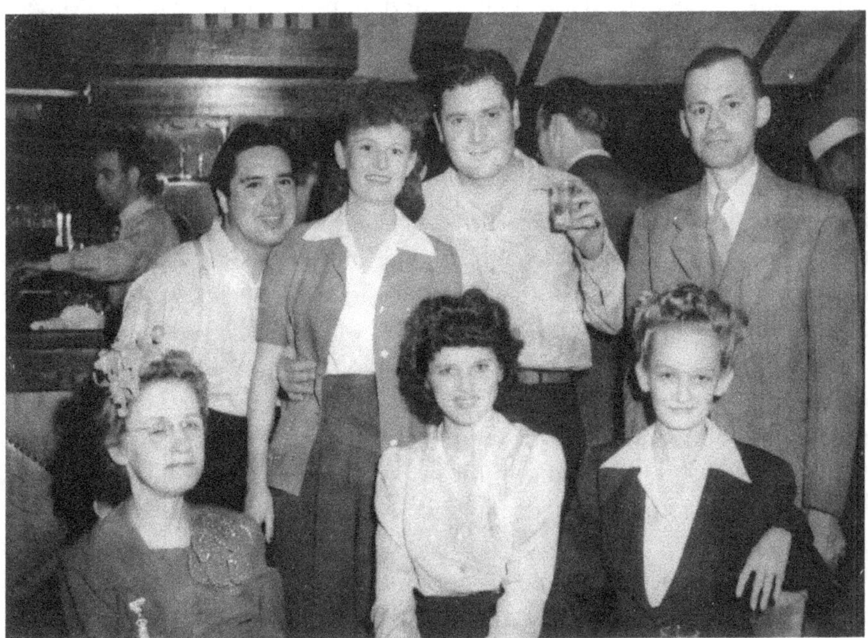

The woman on the far left in this photo has been identified as Mary "Gouch-Eye" Russel, and the girls pictured with her were most likely employees. *Courtesy of Rosenberg Library.*

In addition to her massive fortune, Russel and her sunshine Sallies were a huge advantage for Mayor Cartwright when he was bidding against other port cities for contracts. The two often teamed up to influence business owners and organizational representatives who were considering Galveston as a base of operation. Their most famous triumph involved Lipton Tea, a story that was proudly recalled by Cartwright himself. Eric Fease, a Lipton Tea executive and vice-president of properties, was described as a rather self-righteous and proper Englishman. But the mayor knew that every man has a weakness, just as he knew that Fease was scouting out locations for a new plant. Cartwright cozied up to Fease, who made several trips to the island, where dates with beautiful women were arranged for him. On the day he was traveling to Galveston to sign the contract, Fease insisted that this was a special occasion and he needed a special girl to celebrate.

The mayor immediately called Mary Russel, who had no trouble producing a gorgeous and well-spoken nineteen-year-old from Dallas with old-money class and flawless manners. The plan was to pass her off as a Sunday school teacher, so they took her to Nathan's department store and spent $2,000 on clothing for her to play the part for one weekend. After dinner, Fease whisked her away to the Hotel Galvez, and in the immortal words of Mayor Cartwright, "she must have really put it to him." When the mayor picked up the besotted fellow on Sunday morning, Fease informed him that the girl had gone off to teach Sunday school and that she would be back very soon, so they should hurry and take care of the contracts.[8]

Ruth Kempner was quite possibly the only woman in existence who could marry into Galveston's number one family, play a critical role in overturning the commission government started by her father-in-law and then, instead of being ostracized, make history for a second time. Intelligent, fearless and frank, Ruth Alma Levy married Harris Kempner in 1939. He was the son of Isaac "Ike" Kempner, Galveston's champion after the 1900 storm, whose diligence and dedication to the city's quest to survive complete annihilation is likely the only reason that it did. The commission form of government he installed was designed to give the maximum amount of authority to its members with minimum accountability, which was fine as long as those members were not corrupt.

Ruth became suspect of the system put in place by her husband's father in the late 1950s, around the same time that the illustrious career of Police Commissioner Johnston was in full stride and he was amassing his fortune from coercion. With nothing more than a history degree from the University of Texas, two years as an elementary school teacher and an advantageous marriage on her résumé, Ruth Kempner led an all-out assault on the commission.[9] The feat to amend the city charter to a council-manager form of government required a thorough educational campaign to convince voters why the change was needed, months of rewriting the charter and three elections: one to choose the citizens for the committee to amend the charter, to which Ruth and two other women were elected; the second to approve the council-manager format; and a third to adopt the charter.[10] The opposition was well financed, backed by the elite and powerful men who had survived the storm and thought it incredulous that their contributions to the city were now being undermined. But the charter proposition passed.[11]

Ruth Kempner was not quite finished, however, and she decided to run for a position on the new council in 1961. Her promotion of the new charter had already put her in front of unions, school administrators and employees, houses of worship and even the women of the bawdy houses, for whom she developed a deep level of empathy and respect. She scheduled a campaign appearance with a madam named Big Tit Marie, and their public meeting exuded a feeling of commonality between them despite the stark contrast. Marie was a towering figure with an enormous bosom, adorned in copious amounts of jewelry, makeup and blue brocade, whose bold presence still could not overpower the petite Ruth, who wore a simple cotton dress embellished only with a wedding ring yet spoke boldly and sincerely into the microphone.[12]

> *As far as I'm concerned, but for the grace of God I would be in your house, and I believe that people in your profession have a place, and have always had a place, in our civilization, and I'll do everything in the world I can to protect you, but I want you to know that I intend to have an honest police department....I prefer to live and let live, but if you find that you have to pay off the police, I want to be told about it.*[13]

The red-light district contributed more to her campaign than any other prior candidate,[14] and Ruth Levy Kempner became the first woman elected to Galveston's city government.

9

NOTORIOUS MADAMS

Civil War

Angeline Dickinson

Galveston's first well-known madam rose to Texas fame in the 1860s. They called her the "Babe of the Alamo," because she and her mother were the only white persons to survive the San Antonio slaughter in 1836. Angeline blossomed into a lovely young women with no shortage of suitors, two of whom she married before vying for her own independence. She moved to Galveston to pursue the primrose path, and her presence elicited a deep affection from her clientele. Upon her death at only thirty-four, a Galveston rag called *Flake's Daily Bulletin* printed its condolences: "We do not know how it happened, nor is it necessary to know, but 'the Babe of the Alamo' embraced the life of a courtesan and so died last night. Her pilgrimage is done. Let us erect over her grave the words of a recently departed sister: 'Thou, God, knowest.'"[1]

Cora Morris

Another star of the Civil War days was Cora Morris, a petite girl with perky breasts from Tennessee who served with the Terry's Texas Rangers and made quite a name for herself among ranking members of the Confederacy. When the war was over, Cora moved to Galveston and opened an opulent house that featured long-legged Cajun women who resembled the supermodels of today. It was soon the favorite destination of all of the most distinguished gentlemen, but Cora was also known for her shrewd business sense and compassionate nature.

The astute madam learned shortly after her arrival in Galveston that the premier social event of the year was an artillery ball held at the armory near her house. She knew an opportunity when she saw one, and on the night of the ball, Cora held an open house. Finely clad gentlemen would duck off the dance floor out of sight from their refined ladies and rush over to Cora's for a quick romp before returning to the ballroom.

Cora survived the Great Storm of 1900; in the aftermath, she converted her house into a shelter for women who were injured or had become ill. When a girl in her employ passed away suddenly, Cora mailed out funeral notices to all of the women of the Line instructing them to wear black and not to arrive "under the influence of liquor." No one refused an invitation to Ms. Morris's house, and so the entire population of Galveston prostitutes attended the service led by Dr. S.W. Bird, rector of Trinity Episcopal Church, who preached a powerful sermon titled "The Wages of Sin."[2]

LATE NINETEENTH AND EARLY TWENTIETH CENTURIES

Abbie Allen

Abbie Allen was a madam who went on to marry well and establish her place in high society. She was a blond bombshell, a nationally connected "wholesaler" from California and the madam of an upscale house on the island. Her proficiency in recruiting hot young girls for the sex trade and sending them to all parts of the country, including Galveston, made her one of the few bona fide slave traders in the sex industry. Lurid business practices such as Allen's led to an exaggerated storyline of "white slavery" that was picked up by the propaganda machine of the late nineteenth and early twentieth centuries. She would sell young women to madams for twenty-five dollars apiece. Allen was one of the few proprietors of Galveston prostitution who was able to categorize her professional and personal lives. Outside of working hours, she lived a relatively normal life with her husband, away from the district.[3]

Queen Laura

By far the most majestic procuress of Galveston's early district was Queen Laura, sent to the city by a business associate of Abbie Allen's, a New Orleans madam named Spanish Agnes. Laura was a frequent spectator at the beach racetrack and a regular audience member at lewd burlesque shows, and she was known for her floor-length raven hair that men would pay exorbitant sums to see unfurled from the coif atop her elegant head. She also had a knack for acquiring quite the peculiar assemblage of gentlemen callers. One of her regulars would often arrive unannounced to the Queen's house, banish all of her visitors and lock the door. He would then entertain all of the ladies of the house with an outrageous party. After making her fortune in Galveston, Queen Laura returned to New Orleans to retire.[4]

Jessie Anderson

Another high-profile figure during Queen Laura's day was Jessie Anderson, whose immaculate taste and lavish expenses always sparked rumors of an aristocratic birth. Her clothes came from the finest milliners in New Orleans, and her carriage was drawn by a most impressive group of Thoroughbred horses. Jessie's romantically tragic story was a Postoffice legend that told of a doctor whom she loved passionately and who fully returned her affections. They would often steal away under the cover of his concealed carriage and escape to a ritzy nightclub on the beach called the Halfway House. One night while the pair was enjoying an evening together, Jessie was overcome with an attack of appendicitis. The young doctor rushed her to the hospital and operated on her himself, but she died at his fingertips. After that, he considered his life all but over and drowned himself in drink.[5]

Hazel Harvey

The most maternal of them all was Madam Hazel, known affectionately as Mother Harvey because of her affinity for teaching young men how to "dance." In 1918, Hazel Harvey purchased the 1886 construction at 2528 Postoffice Street, built by Mollie Waters, who had leased the building since her retirement at the turn of the century.[6] Harvey maintained the same level

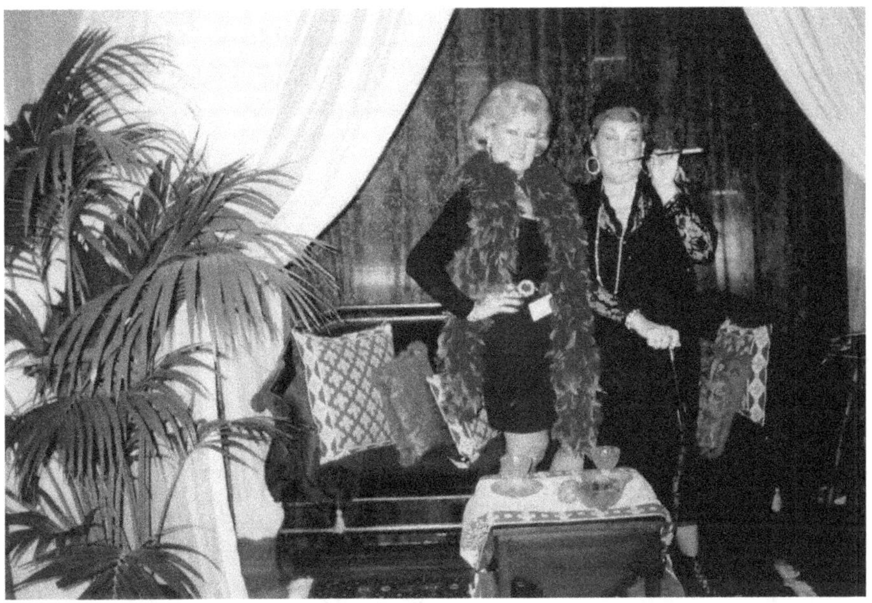

Two docents from the 1992 Homes Tour pose in the hallway of Mother Harvey's house at Twenty-Sixth and Postoffice. *Photo provided anonymously.*

of propriety as had her predecessors, and her sought-after establishment made her a very wealthy woman. Eventually, she left the brothel business and went on to run a successful hotel.[7]

1920s AND '30s

Ardis Smythe

Madam Ardis was a highly intelligent and deeply philosophical woman and an avid reader who became somewhat of a mythic figure on Postoffice Street because of her extremely private nature. She kept to herself within a two-story house across from Twenty-Ninth Street at the edge of the railyard and even installed a second phone line so that her personal calls went directly to her apartment. Known as the "Brick House," it was set apart from the rest of the district, which seemed to suit her natural air of dignity and aloofness. Madam Ardis spoke little of herself and would only ever say she was from somewhere in Texas, but she would not hesitate at all to defend her profession. She stated in an interview, "I have something that men want and are willing to pay for. It's my property, so why shouldn't I sell it? Your goody-goody wives that try to drive us out make me tired. Why can't they see that Galveston's better off with us?"[8]

Madam Janet

Janet was a longtime employee of the Line who made a name for herself years before she opened her own house. Clients saw her as novelty because she practiced "perversion," an anachronistic term for alternate forms of sexual intercourse. In 1927, she decided to open up her own house and made it clear from the beginning that she planned to cater to the "pervert" trade. The concept was an immediate success, and the "French House" became one of the most popular destinations on Postoffice. Janet never took another client after she promoted herself to madam but used her fortune to travel the country and attend World Series baseball games. Even in her later years, when her penchant for whiskey had transformed her into a wrinkly and lumpy lady with straggly hair and gold fillings in her teeth, residents remarked of her continued vivacity as she rushed around the house during business hours, dancing with visitors or flirtatiously demanding money for the Victrola.[9]

Melba Morrison

Another madam who was able to completely distinguish her business life and home life was Melba Morrison. Her dichotomy was inspired by her son, to whom she wanted to be a good mother. When he was old enough to pay attention, she sent him to boarding school in New York. When he would return to Galveston on holidays, Melba would secure lodging in a house by the beach and pretend like it was her home. The lad grew up to become a doctor and never learned the truth about his mother.[10]

Laura Backenstoe

The subject of one of the Line's more tragic tales, Laura was an instant sensation when she began working the Galveston district. She worked her way up to a five-dollar house, but this caused marital strife, and she started using drugs. This negatively impacted her ability to make a living as a girl, and so she started to deal the same drugs she was using. Soon Laura was slapped with federal narcotics charges, but she overdosed on "dream-smoke" three days before her trial.[11]

Lula Wilcox

Lula's stunning red hair was her defining feature, and every head turned when she walked into the room. Her house was located at 2526 Postoffice, next door to Mother Harvey's, and she was listed in the 1940 census as a landlady. She married a rather unassuming man, a squatty Frenchman with curly black hair who had a boisterous personality that helped even the score with Lula's captivating appearance. His cordiality and fatherly approach to Lula's girls and those in surrounding brothels earned him the nickname "Mayor of Postoffice Street." Every year at Christmastime, he would invite his relatives over for dinner at the house. The mayor would take his place at the head of the table, and all of the girls of the house were included in the festivities right alongside the family.[12]

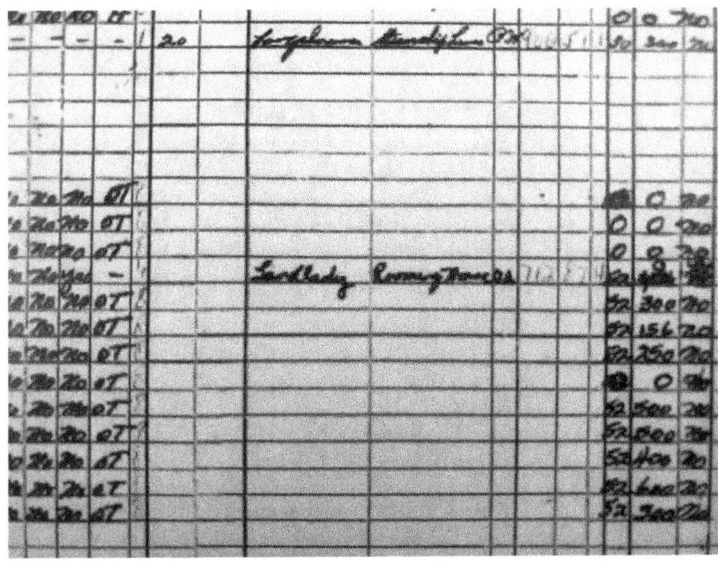

A close-up view of Lula Wilcox's census entry, which reads "Landlady" for her occupation and "rooming house" for the location. *Courtesy of Rosenberg Library.*

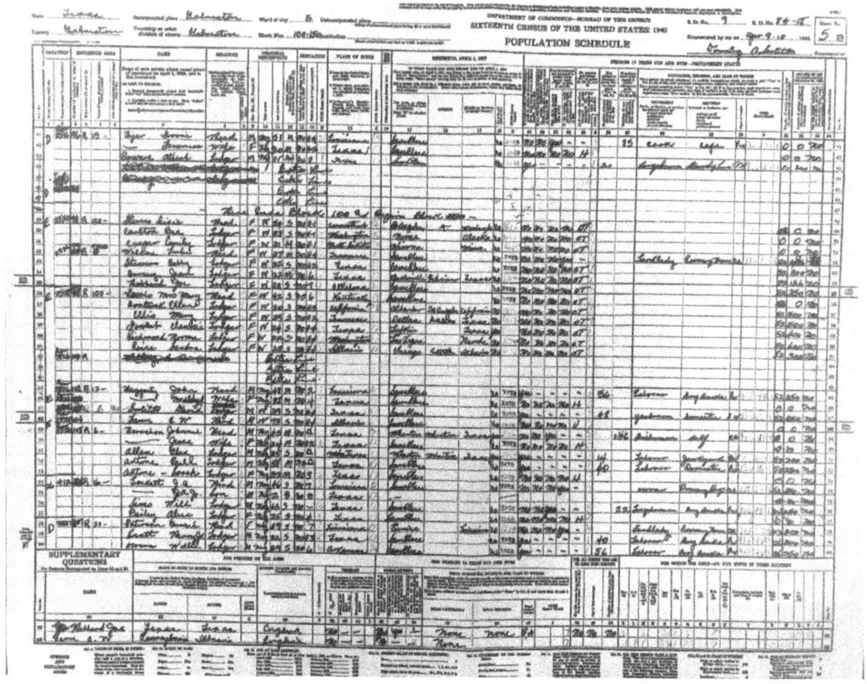

DEPARTMENT OF COMMERCE—BUREAU OF THE CENSUS

SIXTEENTH CENSUS OF THE UNITED STATES: 1940

POPULATION SCHEDULE

SUPPLEMENTARY QUESTIONS

The 1940 Galveston census, which includes known madam Lula Wilcox. *Courtesy of Rosenberg Library.*

1940S AND '50S

Big Foot Mary

The only surviving information about Big Foot Mary besides what can be derived from her colorful nickname is that she was a Spanish madam with a mouth full of diamond-encrusted gold teeth.[13]

Tiger Lil

This exotic beauty was described as having skin like porcelain and the look of a China doll. With an affinity for risqué clothing, Lil was known for her tiger-striped leotards and was said to have been the first woman in Galveston to wear a see-through blouse. She married a pimp, but he was unfaithful, so she shot him. As far as history can tell, she spent the rest of her life in prison.[14]

Jessie "Dirty Neck" Elliot

Perhaps one reason the red-light district in Galveston closed was because no one could have topped Jessie Elliot, who moved to the island after she was banished from Corpus Christi after World War II. Within a handful of years, she had bankrupted the Line's most successful madam up to that point, Mary "Gouch-Eye" Russel, and went on to become the wealthiest madam ever and one of the most powerful people in the city.

When she first moved to Galveston, "Dirty Neck J" was determined to stay out of the bordello business and opened up a nightclub on the outskirts of town. At the time, Sixty-First Street was just outside the city limits and had become a well-populated strip of gambling clubs in the 1930s, the most famous of which was the Hollywood Dinner Club, owned by the Maceos. Jessie wanted to stand out from the other clubs on the street, so she added nude exotic dancers to the equation.

Unfortunately, the street was prone to raids and shutdowns from the Texas Rangers, so in a conundrum that could have existed only in Galveston, Jessie decided that she needed to get into a business that was less troublesome. "I'm tired of violating the law. I'm going to run me a whorehouse," she declared to a business partner, who loaned her the

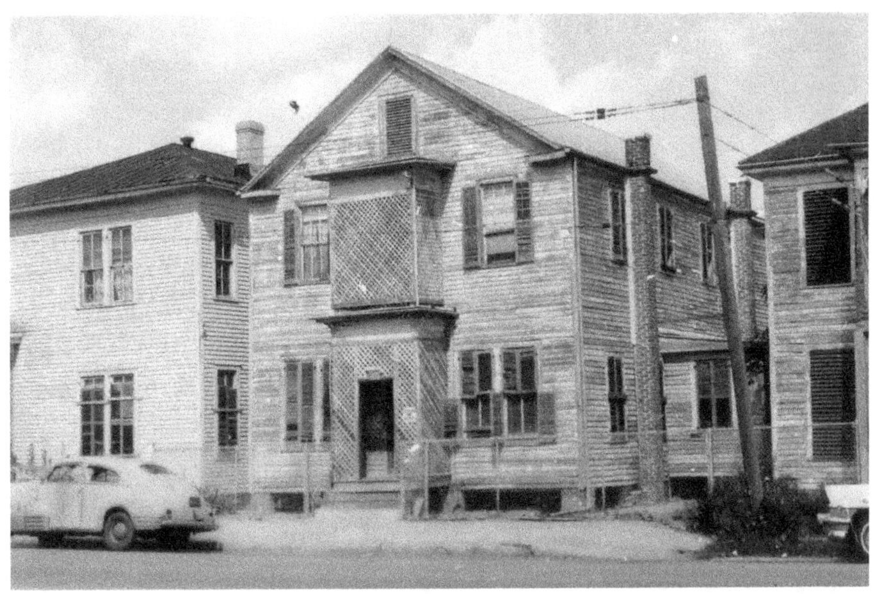

Lula Wilcox's house at 2526 Postoffice Street, circa 1966. *Courtesy Rosenberg Library.*

money to buy a commercial building at Thirty-Seventh Street and the harbor. Dirty Neck J went on to purchase seven more houses, including the Mitzpah Hotel on Twenty-Third Street, another on Twenty-Seventh and three on Postoffice Street.[15] Two of her houses on the Line were connected by a runway, which proved advantageous for her and Mayor Cartwright. When he conducted a "raid" on one house, the girls would scurry over the runway to the other house. After the raid was finished, they would rush back over. Cartwright used this for his own PR and bragged to the papers that he could clear out a house in under five minutes.[16]

Elliot's aggressive expansion of her empire had a dynamic impact on the red-light district of Galveston. The added competition she produced was the reason other madams of the time began to come up with themes and gimmicks for their operations, and Jessie's idea to have girls hawk their services to passersby quickly became standard practice on the Line.[17] Her ability to align herself with political officials such as Cartwright and, later, Mayor Roy Clough made her a fierce player in the strengthening of the district, which prolonged the resistance and exhausted the crusaders.

Part IV

The Girls

10
VICE DOLLS

The madams called them girls. The scholastically minded called them inmates. The newspaper called them vagrants. The mayor called them hogs.[1] They were the dolls of vice, the pretty, powdered faces of an underworld, the soothers of itches and the seekers of thrills. They were counterculture icons of an era in which conformity was aggrandized. They did not set out to be symbols, but history has proven that they were a sign—a sign of dissent against a mass media projection of the ideal woman, the foreshadowing of a movement that would revolutionize the spectrum of options available to females and a statement that the United States would never lose its diversity no matter how many times people tried to cram its identity into a June Cleaver–shaped box.

Willian Acton, a man of science in nineteenth-century Great Britain, proselytized regularly against a depraved archetype of prostitution that he created. "Once a harlot, always a harlot…there is no possible advance, moral or physical, in the condition of the actual prostitute." He also likened prostitution to a microcosm of society, that it exhibits "all the virtues and good qualities, as well as all the vices, weaknesses, and follies."[2] This could not have been truer than it was in Galveston, where the oldest profession became new out of necessity. The vagrants, the inmates and the girls were simply attempting to satiate the voracious demand of this island city—a demand for something that only a woman could supply.

The general timbre of Galveston when the red-light district flourished was much different than its modern incarnation. The city worked hard, and

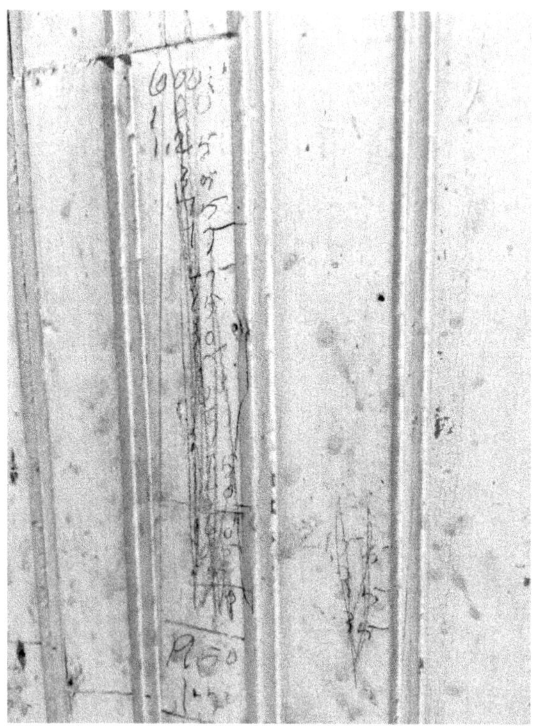

Another nightly tally on the wall of the Oleander. *Photo by author.*

this was reflected in a certain grit and steeliness that was preserved by the facets of its economy. Although today the port of Galveston is relatively well utilized and family-friendly entertainment is the norm, a century ago the city was still the largest cotton port in the world[3] and its entertainment was more focused on the adult demographic. Between 1,500 and 2,000 crew members of various ships would disembark on the island every week,[4] and almost the entire student body of the medical school of the University of Texas on the east end was male. For the first half of the twentieth century, Fort Crockett on the western end of the seawall was a reservation with quarters for the Third Attack Group of the Army Aviation Corps; hundreds of troops moved in and out of the base every week. The Galveston Chamber of Commerce was relentless in pursuit of conventions, which brought an additional 100,000 to 200,000 men to the island each year. Beach attractions included beauty pageants, automobile races, gambling, liquor during Prohibition and illegal liquor by the drink in the decades following, all of which were predominantly male pursuits. The regular and vast procession of men into and around the city, coupled with a time when conquests were limited for young males since sex out of wedlock was considered a definitive transgression for a young woman that could "ruin" her, was undoubtedly a major catalyst for the growth of prostitution in Galveston.[5]

Interestingly, the women on the Line were as transitory as the men passing through the city. Had the madams of Postoffice sought to fill their houses with local girls, the other shoe would have certainly dropped much sooner. A large number of prostitutes working in Galveston came from rural communities of the South and Southwest, and a significant portion represented a number of foreign countries, such as France, Spain and Portugal.[6] Estimations made in the late 1920s revealed that around 60 percent of the girls were American-born white females, with foreign women accounting for another 25 percent and black American women the remaining 15. Some of the girls were sent by national syndicates based in New York, Philadelphia and California. These organizations would actively recruit girls in their area, marking the ones who were in college or working odd jobs as those with an inclination for independence. These recruiting tactics were widely misinterpreted by many as kidnapping, but a survey of the district conducted in 1929 revealed not one inmate had been brought to Galveston against her will.[7]

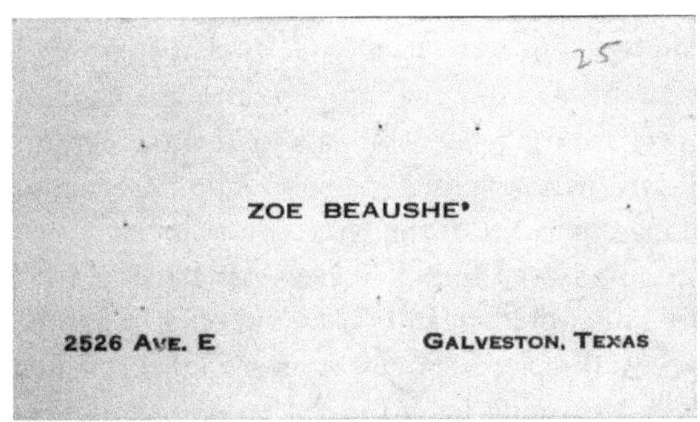

Top: Calling card for Zoe Beaushe', circa 1930. *Courtesy of Rosenberg Library*.

Bottom: The back of Zoe Beaushe's calling card reads, "Sending you $5.00 on [*illegible*], please hold for me, balance $24.50 Miss Zoe Beaushe'." *Courtesy of Rosenberg Library*.

No matter how they got there, a very small percentage of the girls stayed in Galveston permanently or even for an extended amount of time. Prostitutes of the era were often very well-traveled individuals because they were habitually on the move, bouncing between periods of tolerance and intolerance in any given city, chasing the newest district development or simply choosing to live a life of itinerancy because it suited them personally.[8] The girl in this latter category would often work out of hotels in towns that did not have segregated districts, staying for as long as she was tolerated by the hotel staff or until she became bored with the city.[9]

The district was by far the most profitable and economical place for a working girl in Galveston. She was required to pay the madam rent for her crib and 40 percent of her earnings, but these costs were easily offset in brothels where the madams had established names, reputations and clientele. In one evening, a girl could entertain as many as twenty-five johns at a house, and many prostitutes made upward of $420 per week, which equates to more than $5,000 today. Girls would sometimes move from house to house within Galveston; especially if they were a particularly good earner, their prowess could be used to successfully negotiate better terms in a different location.[10]

The number of girls in a house ranged on average from twelve to sixteen, and relationships among them were civil—the madams required any contempt for competition to be kept quiet. Often, however, the madam herself would inadvertently provoke matters if she took fondly to a certain girl or if the house had a "star" who received special treatment because of her beauty or money-making ability.[11] But the typical storyline of every house was one of camaraderie and even fun. If a new girl came in who was frumpy or dirty, the other girls would clean her up and offer to fix her hair or lend her clothing. They would play harmless pranks on their clients, answering telephone calls with a greeting for a funeral home or taunting men out on Postoffice Street by tapping on the parlor room windows.[12]

Such frivolities were needed with a grueling work schedule. Houses were open from 6:00 p.m. to 2:00 a.m. seven days a week, and each girl would work three weeks on and one week off. Each night, they would spend a certain number of hours in the windows and the rest of the time with clients. Frequent revelry helped take the edge off, too. After closing, the housemates along with their pimps and taxi drivers would often venture out to clubs and restaurants that kept certain hours specifically to cater to the girls and their crew, like the Italian diner on the first floor of the Oleander Hotel that was open from 5:00 p.m. to 5:00 a.m.[13] One of the most popular spots among the district workers was the Embassy Club on Twenty-Third Street between

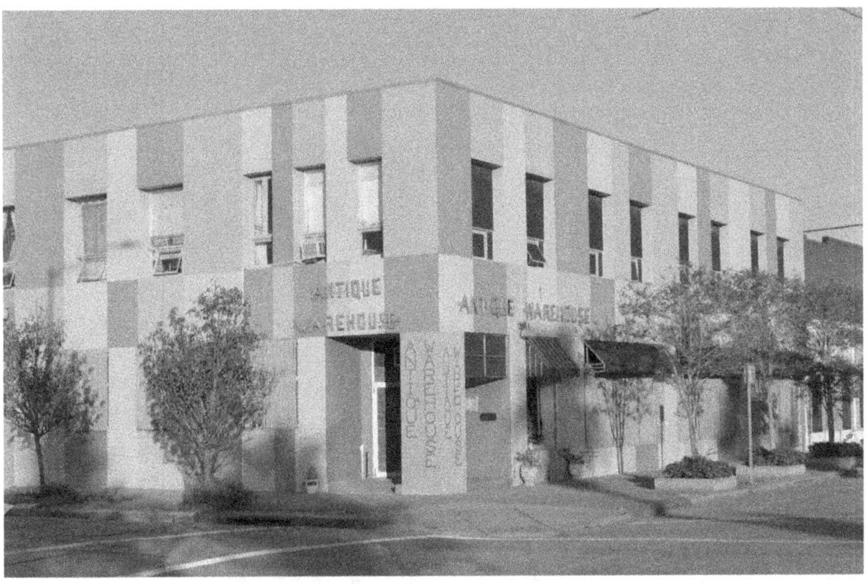

A sign found for an Italian diner was found inside Antique Warehouse (former Oleander Hotel) on the northwest corner of Twenty-Fifth Street and Postoffice and lists its hours as 5:00 p.m. to 5:00 a.m. *Photo by author.*

Market and Postoffice, where the band came on at midnight and played until four o'clock in the morning. Neither the musicians nor the restaurant staff minded the late nights; the girls ordered well, tipped well and always brought a crowd.[14]

Shopkeepers around town were just as delighted as the musicians when they spotted a girl from the Line heading into their store. They were always immaculately dressed and accompanied by either the maid or the madam of the house, and they were loose with their cash. Some of the clothing stores would offer to deliver a sampling of the latest styles directly to the girl's house so she did not have to venture out, and the more established girls even had charge accounts. Merchants at the downtown clothiers never worried about compensation from the women of the district; the bill merely had to be presented and it would promptly be reconciled. In fact, the girls were graciously received almost everywhere they went, because everyone knew they had money to spend. Other daylight activities included regular visits to the salon, trips to the movies and the beach or simply taking a drive in their automobile.[15]

The lifestyle certainly had its upswings, but on occasion the pendulum could easily travel the other direction. Ever-present perils were pregnancy

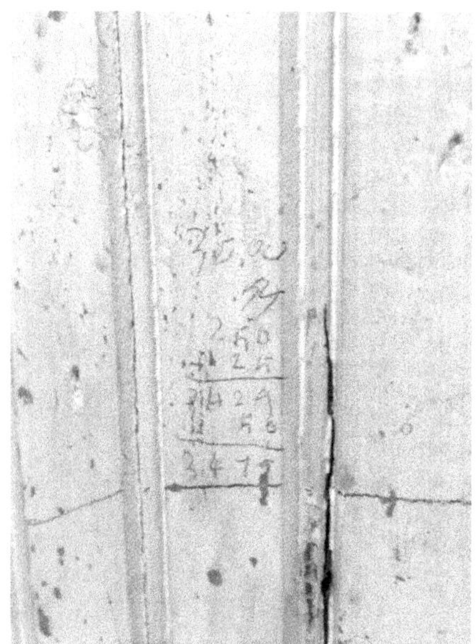

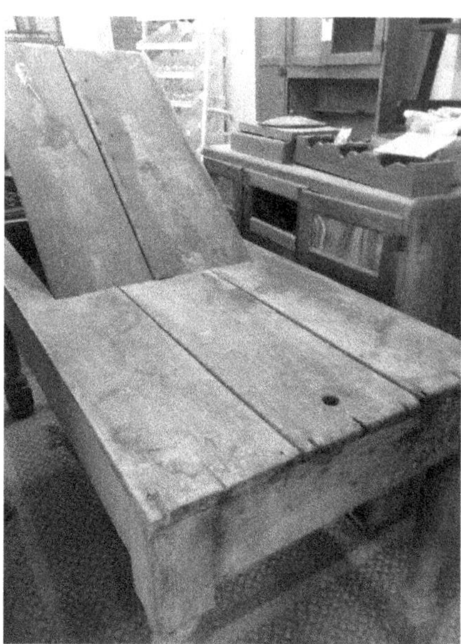

Left: Yet another night's tally found on the wall at Antique Warehouse. *Photo by author.*

Right: This birthing table was found upstairs among the old cribs on the second floor of Antique Warehouse. It was most likely used to perform abortions. *Photo by author.*

and, most common, venereal disease. At the time, diagnoses were often inaccurate and medication was unavailable. In addition to contracting disease, for which girls were said to visit a clinic at Twentieth Street and Mechanic where they would be administered an unknown brown liquid, disease prevention was a major theme of reform groups. To pacify these vociferous protestations, and to give the appearance of a clean district, city officials began to require regular medical examinations and health certificates at the expense of the girl. This system was by no means immune to corruption, however, and it was eventually eliminated.[16]

Police raids were another threat that eternally loomed over every house, madam and girl. Even in times of tolerance, the district was always on call to fatten up city bank accounts whenever the mayor or police chief felt inclined to do so. A single fine could cost each girl up to $25, and if a girl was actually arrested, she was often at the mercy of unscrupulous lawyers who charged them outrageous fees for bonds and representation.[17] A raid or an arrest meant also that the girls could be certain that their names would be published in the newspaper the next day. During periods when the press was a primary weapon in the war against Galveston vice, papers would print reports of staggering inaccuracy from reformers regarding prostitutes,[18] and city officials would blast every last movement in the district to keep up appearances of their diligence. As one girl said cheekily to a reporter as she waited in the police station for her madam to come pay her fine, munching on a candy bar bought for her by the mayor, "Why don't you print this on the society page for a change? We are getting to be celebrities."[19]

11

TARGET PRACTICE

The Postoffice Street district housed one thousand girls at its apex. Considering this substantial presence and the girls' inescapable notoriety, they did not go largely unnoticed. And the ones who did notice most certainly had an opinion. Their good looks and cunning fashion sense were as off-putting to the girls' opponents as they were enticing to their johns. Furthermore, the commonality with polite society afforded to them by their income indicated a level of freedom that was far outside the cultural norm for women at the time. Their monetary gains and independence did nothing to solidify their integrity or validate their choices, however, and instead made them bigger targets and more susceptible to interference from innumerable angles.

Generally, the girls considered themselves outcasts and did not assume themselves equal with polite society, but that was a status coveted by almost every girl on Postoffice. A common theme on the Line was that a girl either had a shiny new car or none—vanity or anonymity, pride in who they were or shame.[1] If a girl possessed pride, her spoils were an avenue for her to feel accepted by the respectable folk. If a girl preferred obscurity, her end was the same, but she was looking farther into the future at her long-term reputation. This explains why, from the perspective of a local resident, the ultimate fate of girls on the Line was that they simply disappeared. A handful died violent, high-profile deaths, and occasionally the paper would report of a suicide at an address on west Postoffice Street. A few girls did remain in Galveston and marry or start legitimate businesses, but for the most part,

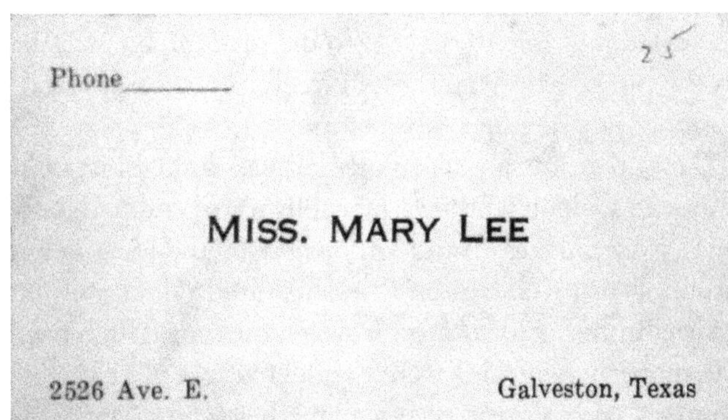
Phone______ 25

MISS. MARY LEE

2526 Ave. E. Galveston, Texas

Calling card for Miss Mary Lee. *Courtesy of Rosenberg Library.*

The back of Mary Lee's calling card reads, "ask for Johnnie." *Courtesy of Rosenberg Library.*

they basically vanished. Most likely, they moved away to seek asylum from their past and make a fresh start.[2] Hopefully, many of them found a place where they could pursue the freedom they sought in Galveston, the city where everyone wanted a piece of them.

Pimps were the most interconnected of the prostitute's predators. The pimp system emerged in the 1920s and saw a sharp increase in the 1930s, perhaps when more men were in need of income during the Depression. The appeal of it was never clear, especially for girls who worked in the district, where the assistance pimps provided was ultimately superfluous.[3] These men often worked elsewhere in the city, usually in the bootlegging or gambling rackets,[4] but a pimp's main duties to his girl were to solicit customers from the gambling parlors and pool halls downtown and to act as an intermediary between the girls and policemen. They were usually close companions to the girls, as well, offering them protection and a promise of stability; but all of these supposed benefits were also fulfilled by most madams. The pimps were always more demanding and controlling than the madams, often setting outrageous quotas for the girls to meet every night.

In addition to the 40 percent to the madam, a cut of the girl's fee also went to the pimp, who would often freely resort to physical abuse if he did not consider her earnings satisfactory.[5]

The press was a particularly ruthless antagonist of the girls on the Line, happy to soak up whatever juicy bits were scrapped to them by the reformers or city officials. Even though owners of the local newspapers were directly profiting from Galveston's underground, all of the news on the red-light district from the local press traveled the moral high road. They commended the mayor when raids were conducted, plainly listed the names of the girls charged with vagrancy the night before and even published astonishing propaganda pieces disguised as medical advice. A doctor from the University of Texas School of Medicine devoted several articles from his "Man vs. Disease" series to prostitution. He concluded one written in 1945 by pleading with his readers to "start thinking and acting with the humane justice and wisdom of a modern society." This was after he had explained to them that most prostitutes are mentally and physically ill, that all prostitutes possess "a feeling of inferiority…low intelligence…and emotional immaturity" and that they "do not make friends; cannot keep jobs; fail in marriage."[6]

Girls were often made to be pawns of politicians and the elite, not only by seducing men to get contracts signed or deals made, but also, on many occasions, the madams with close ties to candidates would offer their girls up to participate in voter-fraud schemes for which they were often arrested.[7] But at least these inconveniences did in some instances do some good, unlike one cringe-worthy account involving a famous bandleader from the 1930s named Phil Harris. He was a good friend of Sam Maceo and a regular performer at his clubs, and one evening Sam suggested that Harris exchange his spotlight for a red light and gave him an address. Shortly after he arrived at the house, it was raided by the police, and all of the girls and Harris were escorted to the police station. Naturally, he called Maceo to bail him out, to which Maceo replied, "Who's this?" Turns out, Sam had set the whole thing up as a prank on Harris.[8] Oddly enough, if Harris had known Galveston, he would have known the whole thing was a setup, because men were never arrested during raids.

On Thursday, May 24, 1956, the *Galveston Daily News* reported that in a bawdy house raid directed by Mayor Clough, six men were arrested "for the first time in the memory of police observers." Eight women were also arrested. The men were charged with loitering in or around a brothel and were listed as businessmen and students who were out-of-towners. The mayor released the students without bond and personally requested that the newspaper not reveal any of the men's identities. The women, on the other hand, received their usual charge of vagrancy and were given fifty-dollar fines; the article listed all of their names.[9]

The most powerful narrative employed by reformers was that the girls were helpless victims of exploitation, a notion affirmed by the 1956 incident but completely contradicted by the girls themselves. Furthermore, the degradation of these women by crusading prohibitionists was in itself a form of exploitation. The reformers used distorted truths to promote their agenda and created caricatures of these women from isolated incidents in an attempt to stultify not what they did but what they symbolized.

12

AN UNLIKELY LEGACY

Early and mid-century prostitutes in Galveston were not symbols of dissent simply because what they did was rebellious, but because of who they were at their core. These were women who were avid readers. They were well traveled and unafraid of venturing out on their own. They dreamed of "spectacular careers" in aviation; some wanted to be authors, nurses or brokers; and all of them wanted to be productive members of society. But they simply could not tolerate the idea of working as a mail clerk or a stenographer. Even less tolerable to them was the idea of marriage.[1] Their inner lives, the very essence of who these girls knew themselves to be flew in the face of everything that the establishment told them was acceptable, and yet they carried on.

It was not simply the orphic visions of a prosperous future that they sought; many of them simply wanted a certain quality of life that was also independent of marriage, and society was such at the time that vagrancy was the only way they could attain it. Even at the lower-end houses, a girl could make more from one customer than she could working an entire day doing general labor like shelling pecans or sewing.[2] Many of the women of Galveston's red-light district had bank accounts, savings accounts, charge accounts, clear titles on automobiles and cash to spend. Therefore, history's aim should not be to explain why these girls became prostitutes but rather to explain why they had no other choice. The reasons they became prostitutes were numerous—left an abusive home, abandoned by their husband, became pregnant, needed college

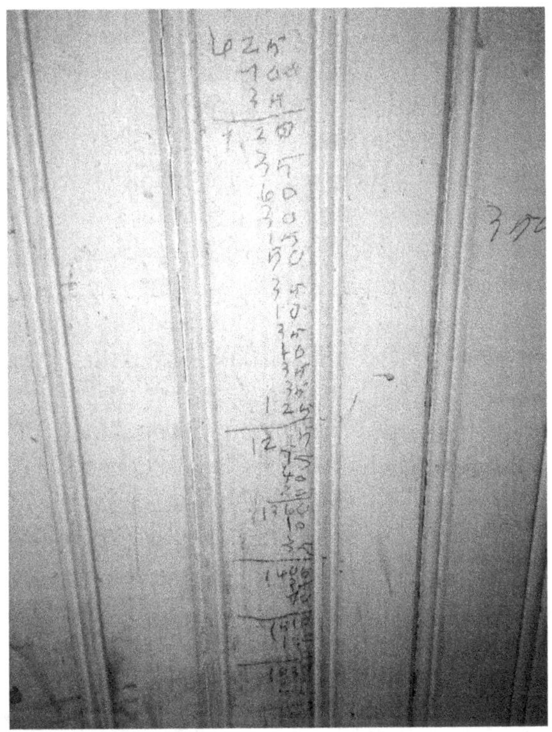

The first segment of this layered tally appears to account for sixteen customers. *Photo by author.*

tuition, wanted a thrill[3]—but there is only one reason that they had no other choice.

Consequently, both the persecution and salvation of these girls was entirely misdirected. The reformers were battling the symptoms and ignoring the disease. If they had truly desired to eliminate or at least reduce prostitution, their efforts would have been much more sustainable had they focused their attention and their pamphlets on educating women on their potential and communities on the premise that a woman can contribute to society in a variety of different ways. This of course would still not have completely done away with the trade, for it is unreasonable to assume that all women disliked the work, but it would have been a much more humane and effective approach. Yet even though this approach was not employed by the anti-prostitution organizations, eventually it was put into play collectively on a much larger scale.

The second-wave feminist movement began to gain momentum in the early 1960s, and among its many endeavors were workplace reform and the sexual revolution. Although direct causation is not quantifiable, the correlation between established gender roles, attitudes toward sex and prostitution was pondered almost a century ago. In his 1925 dissertation for the University of Chicago entitled "The Natural History of Vice Areas in Chicago," W.C. Reckless theorized that the breakdown of "barriers isolating a man's world of the downtown environs from the woman's world of the residential neighborhoods" had actually reduced prostitution in the city. He also attributed the decline to the "individualization" of women and their increased exposure to the outside world, as well as to general changes in people's opinions of extramarital sex. The growing consensus seemed to be that the acceptance of sex with a consenting peer, no matter their marital status, was preferable to seeking out a prostitute and therefore a deterrent to vice.[4]

The most vocal supporters of Galveston's red-light district, most of whom were city and county leaders and elite citizens, argued loudly and often that tolerated prostitution was a benefit to the community. They logically concluded that complete suppression was an impossibility—the demand was a physiological inevitability and some women would always be willing to supply it—and therefore regulation was the only sensible solution. Believers in tolerance also reasoned that prostitution prevented the victimization of respectable girls by providing an outlet for the sexually depraved.[5] At the time, these notions were blasted by the opposing school of thought and deemed ridiculous and ill-informed. Even today, most surveyors of the situation would probably agree that this rationale was nonsensical. However, at one point during the district's presence in Galveston, the police department went eight consecutive years without filing a single rape case,[6] and modern legislative incubators have revealed and proven the viability of the arguments made by vice-loving islanders sixty years ago.

Since the days of the red-light district, every state in the United States with the exception of Nevada has made prostitution illegal. Yet between 70,000 and 80,000 people are arrested in the United States every year for prostitution, sex trafficking is an epidemic and sex workers are reported to be violently assaulted at least once a month.[7] Prohibition has proven ineffective, and sadly, many sex workers who are victims of violence never report their attacker out of fear of being prosecuted for their own indiscretions. This enigma has prompted a wave of twenty-first-century reform throughout Europe, and the concept is slowly gaining momentum in the United States.

Policy reforms in Great Britain (1959), Nevada (1971), Sweden (1999), Denmark (1999), the Netherlands (2000), Germany (2002), New Zealand (2003), Norway (2009), Taiwan (2009), Canada (2012) and France (2016)

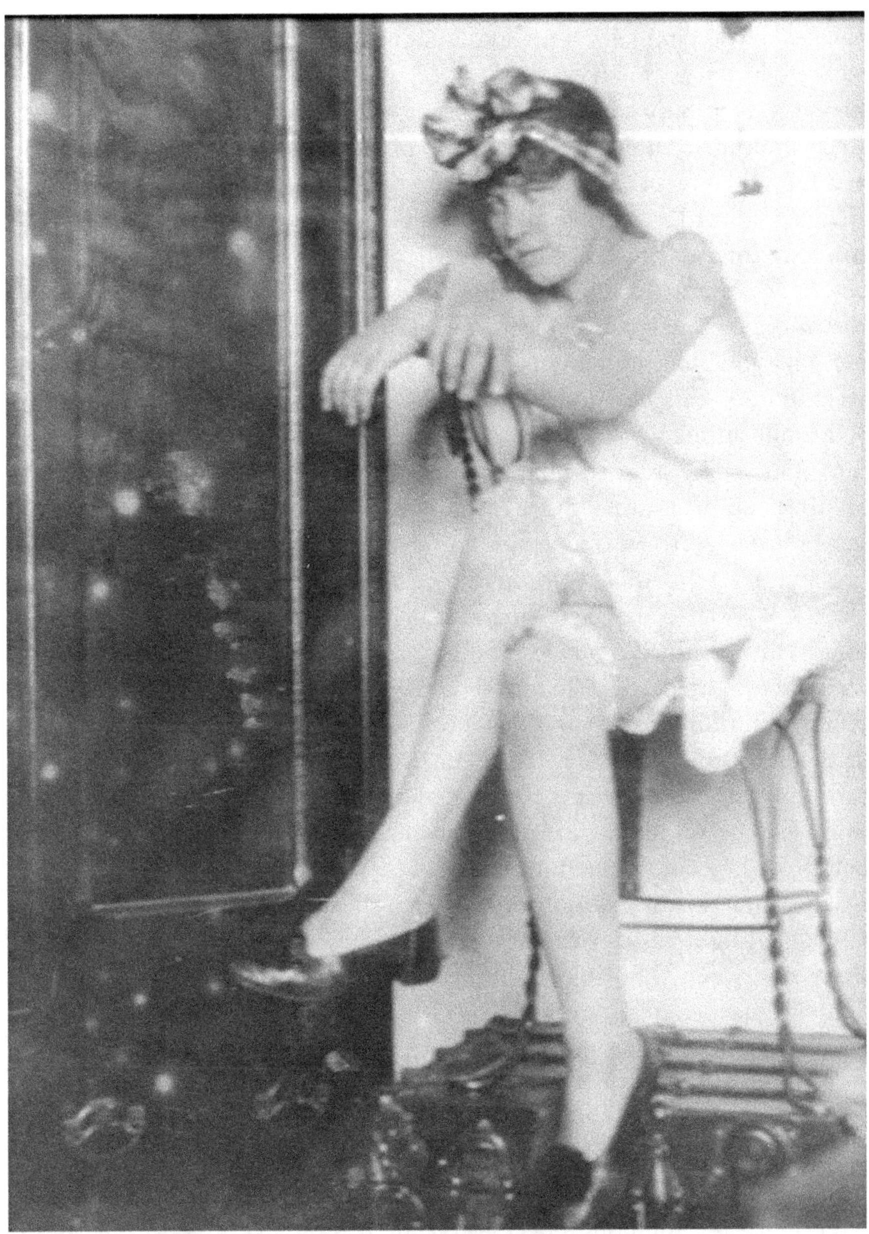

This is the only surviving photograph from a collection discovered inside Mother Harvey's years after it was abandoned. The rest of the photographs, which were originally hung on the walls of the parlor for men to peruse, were destroyed in Hurricane Ike. *Personal collection of Trey Click.*

have either decriminalized prostitution, legalized brothels or made the sale of sex but not its purchase legal, all of which are intended to remove the stigma from prostitution and encourage sex-worker victims of violence to feel comfortable coming forward.[8] Hawaii also considered decriminalization in 2007, and it is currently on the table in Washington, D.C., but the biggest advance toward rewriting the narrative about prostitution came from Amnesty International on May 25, 2016, when it released its long-awaited new policy on the decriminalization of sex work.

Amnesty International is a London-based nongovernmental organization that campaigns to end abuses on human rights, and the formation of this new policy was inspired by the disproportionate level of assault on sex workers and a recent increase in sex trafficking around the globe. The report unabashedly promoted the decriminalization of prostitution, touting this as the best tactic to reduce violence in the sex industry, curb underage prostitution and reduce trafficking. In an explanatory note that accompanies the policy, Amnesty International clearly elucidates the facts surrounding decriminalization and outlines how it can effectively assuage the inhumane practice of selling women and girls into the sex trade. Current data has revealed that the determination of prostitution as illegal does nothing whatsoever to deter human trafficking. On the other hand, decriminalization provides a greater assistance to these victims and supplements anti-trafficking initiatives, since fear of criminal charges often deters many victims from seeking help from law enforcement officials.[9]

The final historical outpouring that flows forth from Galveston's fabled red-light district is one that is doubly powerful, because it was shared between the girls of the Line and the city itself: a legacy of fiercely guarded independence. According to both Galveston and its gals, freedom was the most valuable attribute of human existence one could possess—more treasured than social acceptance, and even more important than obeying the law. They knew that everyone would not like what they were doing, but they also knew that those same people had a choice whether or not to visit them and partake in what they had to offer. Placating someone's aversion to their existence was not the moral responsibility of the city, nor was it the girls'—indeed, both were well aware that they had a responsibility only to themselves.

Appendix A

MAP OF DOWNTOWN GALVESTON AND THE LINE

Although Galveston's segregated district was technically relegated to 6 blocks of Postoffice Street, this map of the downtown area strategically includes certain houses to reveal that, at its peak, the district spanned nearly 150 square blocks of the city and was seamlessly intermingled with official government buildings. All houses west of Twenty-Sixth Street on the Line have been demolished.

Note: Galveston is plotted on a grid: streets running east to west are numbered in ascending order traveling westward, streets running north to south begin with Avenue A on the northern edge of the island (also known as Harborside Drive, located on the very top of the map) and travel alphabetically in a southerly direction.

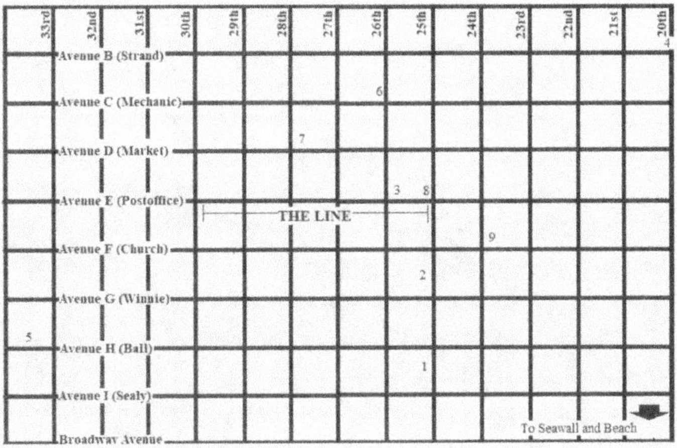

Appendix A

1. City Hall
2. Former Customhouse/Courthouse/Post Office Building
3. Mother Harvey's (2628 Postoffice Street)
4. The Rainbow Room (116 Twentieth Street)
5. Former brothel that is currently a residence (3311 Ball Street)
6. Last known Galveston brothel, in operation until the 1990s (201 Twenty-Sixth Street, currently Havana Alley Cigar Shop & Lounge)
7. This block of Market Street was home to several brothels after the Line was officially shut down in 1953 (2701 Market, currently home to Daiquiri Time Out, 2727 Market (vacant) and 2713 Market (demolished))
8. Former Oleander Hotel (423 Twenty-Fifth Street, currently Antique Warehouse)
9. One of the few buildings erected specifically to be a brothel (2325 Church Street, currently a bar called the Wizzard)

Appendix B

ADDRESSES OF KNOWN BORDELLOS

Houses owned by Mary "Gouch Eye" Russel

Twenty Club, 2520 Postoffice (demolished)
2526 Postoffice (demolished)

Houses owned by Jessie "Dirty Neck" Elliot

2602 Postoffice (demolished)
2606 Postoffice (demolished)
Twelve Club, 2612 Postoffice (demolished)
Mirror Club, 2620 Postoffice (demolished)
Mizpah Hotel, Twenty-Third Street (exact location unknown, demolished)
Mississippi House, 2713 Church (demolished)

Other Known Addresses

Bristol Hotel, 2015½ Postoffice
Lamplighter Club, 2507 Postoffice (demolished)

Oleander Hotel, 2506 Postoffice Street (current address 422 Twenty-Fifth Street)
Twenty Eight Club, 2528 Postoffice (also known as Mother Harvey's)
Hilarity Club, 2701 Postoffice Street (demolished)
Twenty Seven O Five Club, 2705 Postoffice Street (demolished)
Pleasure Club, 2709 Postoffice Street (demolished)
Twenty Seven Club, 2710 Postoffice Street (demolished)
Seventy Two Club, 2720 Postoffice Street (demolished)
Morris Ray House, 2722 Postoffice Street (demolished)
The Embassy Club, 2320 Postoffice Street (demolished)
Margaret's Tea Room, 711 Twenty-Ninth Street (demolished)
The Rainbow Room, 116 Twentieth Street
2616 Postoffice Street (demolished)
2805 Postoffice (demolished)
2709½ Market Street
2714½ Market Street (demolished)
2727 Market Street
2325 Church Street
201 Twenty-Sixth Street
3311 Ball Street

*Business names listed above are according to city directories from the 1920s to the 1950s

Remaining Brothels Listed in 1967 ASHA Survey

True Friends Bar, 2619½ Market
Show Place Bar & Grill, 2701 Market Street
Rio Grande Club, 2713 Market Street (demolished)
Silver Dollar Bar & Lounge, 114 Twentieth Street
Hugo's #2 Tavern, 405 Twenty-Fourth Street
Two Friends Tavern, 313 Twenty-Fifth Street (demolished)
Lafitte's Bar & Lounge 305 Twenty-Fifth Street (demolished)
419 Twenty-Seventh Street

NOTES

Chapter 1

1. Waldman, "Isle," 23.
2. Humphrey, "Prostitution in Texas," 27.
3. Kilman, "Galveston's Street of Shame," 567.
4. Waldman, "Isle," 23.
5. Brown, "Free Rein," 3–4.
6. Ibid, 4.
7. Ibid, 4.
8. Ibid, 5.
9. Kilman, "Galveston's Street of Shame," 568.
10. Ibid, 569.
11. Brown, "Free Rein," 5.
12. Turner, *Women*, 24.
13. Johnson, "Galveston in the Good Old Days."
14. Kilman, "Galveston's Street of Shame," 569.

Chapter 2

1. Humphrey, "Prostitution in Texas," 28.
2. Ibid., 30.
3. Brown, "Free Rein," 6.
4. Ibid., 91.
5. Price, "Sociological Study," 72–73.
6. Ibid., 92.
7. *Galveston Daily News*, August 7, 1917.
8. Price, "Sociological Study," 7.

9. Brown, "Free Rein," 93.
10. Butler, *Daughters of Joy*, 124.
11. Price, "Sociological Study," 68.
12. Ibid., 70.
13. Ibid., 71.
14. Ibid., 29.
15. Ibid., 86–87.
16. Ibid., 6.
17. Waldman, "Isle," 38.
18. "Introduction," *1932 Galveston City Directory*, 13.
19. Kilman, "Galveston's Street of Shame," 574.
20. Humphrey, "Prostitution in Texas," 34.
21. Keedy, "Venereal Disease."
22. *Galveston Daily News*, February 18, 1944.
23. Frazier, "Man vs. Disease."
24. Brown, "Free Rein," 99.

Chapter 3

1. Humphrey, "Prostitution in Texas," 35.
2. Ibid., 36.
3. Turner, *Women*, 290.
4. "Galveston: Open City," *Eye Magazine*, January 1952, 17.
5. Interview, anonymous, September 27, 2017.
6. "Galveston: Open City," *Eye Magazine*, January 1952, 16.
7. Waldman, "Isle," 37.
8. "Galveston: Open City," *Eye Magazine*, January 1952, 17.
9. To put the size of the Maceo empire in perspective for the reader, the average gross yearly income of Al Capone in the 1920s was $100 million per year.
10. The name of the organization was changed to the American Social Health Association in 1960.
11. Lillian E. Herz, "Mayor to Step Up Raids," *Galveston Daily News*, February 2, 1956.
12. "Prostitution in Galveston," American Social Hygiene Association, Folder 110:1.
13. Ibid., Folder 110:5.
14. Ibid., Folder 110:1.
15. Ibid., Folder 110:2.
16. Ibid., Folder 110:5.
17. Ibid.
18. Ibid.
19. "Grand Jury Probe," *Baytown Sun*, December 8, 1953.
20. "Galveston Prostitution Ring Broken," Associated Press, December 29, 1954.
21. "Prostitution in Galveston," American Social Hygiene Association, Folder 110:6.
22. "Proceedings of September 23, 1955," Galveston Chamber of Commerce Records.

23. "Prostitution in Galveston," American Social Hygiene Association, Folder 110:6.
24. Clough, "Why I Want Galveston."
25. "Proceedings of September 23, 1955." Galveston Chamber of Commerce Records.
26. "Vice Dolls," *New York Post*, July 26, 1955.
27. "Wide-Open Galveston Mocks Texas Laws," *Life*, August 15, 1955.
28. "Proceedings of September 23, 1955." Galveston Chamber of Commerce Records.
29. Clough, "Why I Want Galveston."
30. Herz, "Mayor."
31. "Mayor Leads,'" *Galveston Daily News,* May 24, 1956.
32. "Prostitution in Galveston," American Social Hygiene Association, Folder 110:8.
33. Ibid.
34. "Vice Crackdown," *Corpus Christi Times*, July 20, 1957.
35. Remmers, *Going Down the Line*, 11.
36. "Prostitution in Galveston," American Social Hygiene Association, Folder 110:8.
37. Ibid.
38. Interview, anonymous, September 27, 2017.
39. "Prostitution in Galveston," American Social Hygiene Association, Folder 110:8.
40. "Bares Isle," *Galveston Daily News*, April 20, 1960.
41. "Commercialized Prostitution," American Social Health Association, March 1967.

Chapter 4

1. Brown, "Free Rein," 4.
2. Remmers, *Going Down the Line*, 9.
3. Price, "Sociological Study," 2–4.
4. Ibid., 6.
5. Remmers, *Going Down the Line*, 5.
6. *1954 Galveston City Directory*.
7. *1949 Galveston City Directory*.
8. Price, "Sociological Study," 26.
9. Ibid., 29.
10. Ibid., 37.
11. Ibid., 9.
12. Remmers, *Going Down the Line*, 7.
13. Ibid., 7; "Commercialized Prostitution," American Social Health Association, March 1967.
14. Interview, anonymous, December 15, 2017.
15. Remmers, *Going Down the Line*, 7.
16. Ibid.

Chapter 5

1. Remmers, *Going Down the Line*, 6.
2. Waldman, "Isle," 38–39.
3. Remmers, *Going Down the Line*, 7.
4. Brown, "Free Rein," 93.
5. Remmers, *Going Down the Line*, 5.
6. Price, "Sociological Study," 16.
7. Waldman, "Isle," 46.
8. Price, "Sociological Study," 36–37.
9. Remmers, *Going Down the Line*, 15.
10. Waldman, "Isle," 46.
11. Brown, "Free Rein," 102.
12. Kilman, "Galveston's Street of Shame," 572.
13. Brown, "Free Rein," 102.
14. Waldman, "Isle," 41.
15. Kilman, "Galveston's Street of Shame," 572.
16. Waldman, "Isle," 39.
17. Price, "Sociological Study," 53.
18. Kilman, "Galveston's Street of Shame," 573.
19. Brown, "Free Rein," 102.
20. Ibid.
21. Waldman, "Isle," 39, 48.
22. Remmers, *Going Down the Line*, 20.

Chapter 6

1. Price, "Sociological Study," 7.
2. Waldman, "Isle," 38.
3. Annual income per house based on the estimate of $20,000 per week (Remmers, *Going Down the Line*, 7); comparison based on the Crime Commission's revelation of Maceos' annual income for the year 1950 (chapter 3). Dollar amounts have not been adjusted for inflation.
4. Brown, "Free Rein," 99.
5. Interview, anonymous, September 27, 2017.
6. Ibid.
7. Interview, Lee Carson, December 20, 2017.
8. Interview, Scotty Hanson, February 17, 2017.
9. "Commercialized Prostitution," American Social Health Association, March 1967.

Chapter 7

1. Price, "Sociological Study," 40.
2. Ibid., 41.

3. Remmers, *Going Down the Line*, 6.
4. Interview, Scotty Hanson, February 17, 2016.
5. Price, "Sociological Study," 36.
6. Ibid., 37.
7. Remmers, *Going Down the Line*, 7, 18, 19–20.
8. Ibid., 19, 22.
9. Waldman, "Isle," 41.
10. Remmers, *Going Down the Line*, 16.
11. Ibid., 7.
12. "Commercialized Prostitution," American Social Health Association, March 1967.
13. Price, "Sociological Study," 11.
14. Ibid., 12.
15. Ibid., 11.
16. "Mayor Leads,'" *Galveston Daily News*, May 24, 1956.
17. Interview, Scotty Hanson, February 17, 2016.
18. Price, "Sociological Study," 38.
19. Remmers, *Going Down the Line*, 19.

Chapter 8

1. Kilman, "Galveston's Street of Shame," 572.
2. Waldman, "Isle," 43.
3. Ibid., 41.
4. Remmers, *Going Down the Line*, 21.
5. Price, "Sociological Study," 9.
6. Waldman, "Isle," 49.
7. Brown, "Free Rein," 98–99.
8. Waldman, "Isle," 44–45.
9. Stephens, *Matriarch*, 353.
10. "Mrs. Kempner Isle Civic Booster," *Galveston Daily News*, September 12, 1965.
11. Cartwright, *Galveston*, 290.
12. Stephens, *From Matriarch*, 367–368.
13. 1981 interview with Ruth Kempner, as recorded in Stephens, *From Matriarch*, 367–68.
14. Cartwright, *Galveston*, 291.

Chapter 9

1. Kilman, "Galveston's Street of Shame," 568.
2. Ibid., 568–69.
3. Ibid., 570.
4. Ibid., 570–71.
5. Ibid., 571–72.

6. Remmers, *Going Down the Line*, 9.
7. Kilman, "Galveston's Street of Shame," 573.
8. Price, "Sociological Study," 5, 45.
9. Ibid., 46–47.
10. Kilman, "Galveston's Street of Shame," 572.
11. Ibid., 573.
12. Ibid.
13. Remmers, *Going Down the Line*, 8.
14. Ibid., 14.
15. Brown, "Free Rein," 101–2.
16. Waldman, "Isle," 45.
17. Brown, "Free Rein," 102.

Chapter 10

1. Clough, "Why I Want Galveston."
2. William Acton as quoted in Bell, *Reading, Writing*, 53.
3. Price, "Sociological Study," 17.
4. Waldman, "Isle," 42.
5. Price, "Sociological Study," 17–25.
6. Remmers, *Going Down the Line*, 9.
7. Price, "Sociological Study," 14–15.
8. Humphrey, "Prostitution in Texas," 29.
9. Price, "Sociological Study," 44.
10. Ibid., 38.
11. Ibid., 36.
12. Remmers, *Going Down the Line*, 18–20.
13. Interview, Scotty Hanson, February 17, 2016.
14. Brown, "Free Rein," 100.
15. Price, "Sociological Study," 37.
16. Remmers, *Going Down the Line*, 11.
17. Price, "Sociological Study," 32.
18. Frazier, "Man vs. Disease."
19. "Mayor Leads," *Galveston Daily News*, May 24, 1956.

Chapter 11

1. Price, "Sociological Study," 3.
2. Ibid., 41.
3. Remmers, *Going Down the Line*, 20.
4. Price, "Sociological Study," 26.
5. Remmers, *Going Down the Line*, 10, 20.
6. Frazier, "Man vs. Disease."

7. "Prostitution in Galveston," American Social Hygiene Association, Folder 110:1.
8. Brown, "Free Rein," 94–95.
9. "Mayor Lead," *Galveston Daily News*, May 24, 1956.

Chapter 12

1. Price, "Sociological Study," 42.
2. Humphrey, "Prostitution in Texas," 33.
3. Price, "Sociological Study," 16.
4. Reckless, *The Natural History*, as quoted in Price, "Sociological Study," 103.
5. Price, "Sociological Study," 72.
6. Waldman, "Isle," 42.
7. "Prostitution," Legal Resources, www.HG.org.
8. "History of Prostitution," www.ProCon.org.
9. "Amnesty International Policy on State Obligations," 2016.

BIBLIOGRAPHY

Books

1932 Galveston City Directory. Galveston, TX: Morrison & Fourmy Directory Company, 1932.

1939 Galveston City Directory. Galveston, TX: Morrison & Fourmy Directory Company, 1939.

1941 Galveston City Directory. Galveston, TX: Morrison & Fourmy Directory Company, 1941.

1949 Galveston City Directory. Galveston, TX: Morrison & Fourmy Directory Company, 1949.

1954 Galveston City Directory. Galveston, TX: Morrison & Fourmy Directory Company, 1954.

Abbot, Karen. *Sin in the Second City*. New York: Random House, 2007.

Bell, Shannon. *Reading, Writing, and Rewriting the Prostitute Body*. Bloomington and Indianapolis: Indiana University Press, 1994.

Butler, Anne M. *Daughters of Joy, Sisters of Misery*. Urbana and Chicago: University of Illinois Press, 1987.

Cartwright, Gary. *Galveston: A History of the Island*. Fort Worth, TX: Texas Christian University Press, 1991.

Remmers, Mary W. *Going Down the Line*. Galveston, TX: Mary Remmers, 1997.

Ringdal, Nils Johan. *Love for Sale*. New York, NY: Grove Press, 1997.

Stephens, Elise Hopkins. *From Matriarch to Mayor*. Houston, TX: Bright Sky Press, 2016.

Turner, Elizabeth Hayes. *Women, Culture, and Community: Religion and Reform in Galveston, 1880–1920*. New York: Oxford University Press, 1997.

Newspaper and Magazine Articles

Associated Press. "Galveston Prostitution Ring Broken." December 29, 1954.

Baytown Sun. "Grand Jury Probe of Galveston." December 8, 1953.

Cartwright, Gary. "One Last Shot." *Texafs Monthly*, June 1993.

Clough, George Roy. "Why I Want Galveston an Open Town." *Man's Magazine* 3, no. 7 (October 1955).

Corpus Christi Times. "Vice Crackdown May Spread." July 20, 1957.

Frazier, Dr. Chester North. "Man vs. Disease," Fourth in series. *Galveston Daily News*, October 28, 1945.

———. "Man vs. Disease," *Galveston Daily News*, November 4, 1945.

Galveston Daily News. "Mayor Leads More Raids on 'Houses.'" May 24, 1956.

———. "Mrs. Kempner Isle Civic Booster." September 12, 1965.

———. "Vice Squad Raid Nets Five Women." February 18, 1944.

Galveston Tribune. "Bares Isle, But Not San Antonio, Houston Prostitution Survey Data." April 20, 1960.

"Galveston: Wide-Open Sin Town." *Tempo*, June 13, 1955.

Heller, Mike. "Galveston: Open City of Sin." *Eye People and Pictures*, January 1952.

Herz, Lillian E. "Mayor Will 'Step Up' Raids on 'Houses.'" *Galveston Daily News*, February 15, 1956.

———. "This is Galveston: The First City Council." *Galveston Daily News*, April 16, 1961.

Humphrey, David C. "Prostitution in Texas: From the 1830s to the 1960s." *East Texas Historical Journal* 33, issue 1, Article 8, 1995.

Keedy, Carlton. "Venereal Disease Infection Is Still Big Problem for Military." *Galveston Daily News*, January 9, 1943.

Kilman, Ed. "Galveston's Street of Shame." *American Mercury*, May 1942.

Kirkpatrick, Joel. "Two Alleged Bawdy Houses Hit in Raid by Texas Rangers." *Galveston Daily News*, September 23, 1969.

Life. "Wide-Open Galveston Mocks Texas Laws." August 15, 1955.

New York Post. "Vice Dolls Face the Bum's Rush in Galveston." July 26, 1955.

Waldman, Alan. "Isle of Illicit Pleasures: Prostitution." *In Between*. September 27, 1983.

Theses and Dissertations

Brown, Jean M. "Free Rein: Galveston Island's Alcohol, Gambling, and Prostitution Era, 1839–1957." Master's thesis, College of Graduate Studies at Lamar University, August 1998.

Price, Granville. "A Sociological Study of a Segregated District." Master's thesis, University of Texas at Austin, June 1930.

Reckless, W.C. "The Natural History of Vice Areas in Chicago." Dissertation, University of Chicago, 1925.

Articles in an Online Journal

"History of Prostitution from 2400BC to Present." www.ProCon.org.

Johnson, Jan. "Galveston in the Good Old Days: Infamous Postoffice Street." www.TwistedParrot.com/ prostitutionpart1.

"Prostitution in the United States." Legal Resources. www.HG.org.

Papers Presented in a Meeting or Conference

"Amnesty International Policy on State Obligations to Respect, Protect and Fulfill the Human Rights of Sex Workers." Amnesty International, London, May 26, 2016.

"The Case against the Red Light." Issued by the United States Public Health Service in cooperation with the State Board of Health, Richmond, Virginia, 1923.

"Commercialized Prostitution Conditions in Galveston, Texas and Environs." American Social Health Association, March 1967.

"Proceedings of September 23, 1955." Galveston Chamber of Commerce Records.

"Prostitution in Galveston, Texas." Documents from 1949–1960 selected from boxes 109–110 in the American Social Health Association Records. Social Welfare History Archives, University of Minnesota Libraries, 1992.

Interviews

Anonymous. Interview with the author. September 27, 2017.

Anonymous. Interview with the author. December 15, 2017.

Carson, Lee. Interview with the author. December 20, 2017.

Field, Scott. Interview with the author. October 21, 2017.

Hanson, Scotty. Interview with the author. February 17, 2016.

ABOUT THE AUTHOR

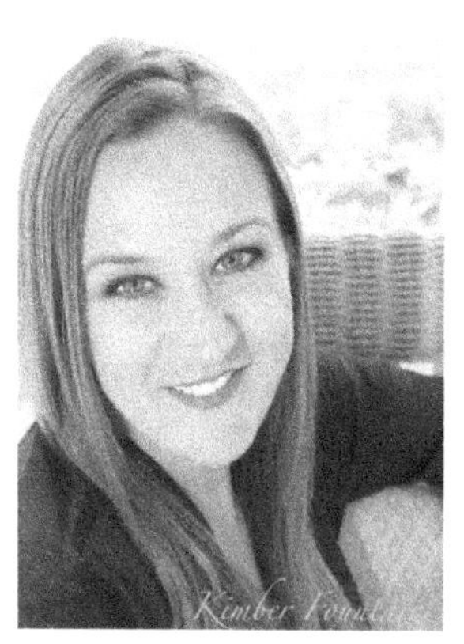

Kimber Fountain is a native of the Texas Gulf Coast and a longtime resident of Galveston Island. After earning a bachelor of arts degree in theatre and dance from the University of Texas at Austin, she lived in Chicago for several years before moving to the island, where she soon discovered a love for the city's history while working as a tour guide on the Strand. Currently, Kimber is the editor-in-chief of *Galveston Monthly* magazine, where she has been a feature writer since 2015. She also serves as chair of the Arts & Historic Preservation Advisory Board to the Galveston City Council and performs with the Island East-End Theatre Company in downtown Galveston. This is Kimber Fountain's second book from The History Press; *Galveston Seawall Chronicles* was released in May 2017.